BOHEMIAN
MOMÉ

Bohemian Momé

A JOURNEY OF DISCOVERY AND RECOVERY

Patti Zona

ISBN: 978-621-434-133-7 (softcover)
         978-621-434-134-4 (hardcover)
         978-621-434-135-1 (eBook)

Printed in New York by:

OMNIBOOK CO.
99 Wall Street, Suite 118
New York, NY 10005
USA
+1-866-216-9965
www.omnibookcompany.com

First Edition

For e-book purchase: Kindle on Amazon, Barnes and Noble
Book purchase: Amazon.com, Barnes & Noble, and
www.omnibookcompany.com

Omnibook titles may be purchased in bulk for educational, business, fund-raising, or sales promotional use. For more information please e-mail **info@omnibookcompany.com**

Designed by: Gian Carlo Tan

CONTENTS

DEDICATION

As difficult as this book was to write, once more I feel such gratitude. For I appreciate the encouragement and support given when coming from a weary state of being. This is my third book. Memories of my first dedication to give was filled with such hope, yet a certain amount of fear and trepidation. I didn't want to offend or hurt anyone. So, I tread softly, gently but I approached the subject with determination to inspire and awaken the conscience. I honestly believed, if read and understood in the sincerity written-- lives could be changed for the better. We continually keep learning when healthy in mind, body and spirit. For a reason that is greater than we can understand at that moment in time. Therefore, patience is a virtue that in this world of access and excess is not always recognized or appreciated.

Now, when I wrote my second book. I was somewhat angry and disappointed too. For, some did not want my book out there. But they could not have read that book. For if they did, they would have nothing to fear. In fact, it might have created more of an awareness in actions and transparency in transactions. The importance of knowing the possibilities and outcome, trust to be honest and fair in offering the best service or product possible. Keep integrity, respect and quality in your daily life at home, work and abroad. For you represent your family, your community and society here and there. Be and give the best of yourself. Others will follow. If not now, later-- when they understand we are in this world together. We all have a reason and purpose. Let's find it and make it for the good for all. No one is to suffer from broken promises and forgotten dreams. We can achieve and accomplish great things when we understand where we are coming from and where we are going. Our future is at stake when we replace or misplace. Will we learn the lesson well or the hard way? Or, will we learn at all?

After all I went through and after all is said and done I still have gratitude. Life is a journey of discovery and recovery. The unique thing about this book brought a newfound incentive and interest. For that I am thankful. Whatever I write I will continue to dedicate my writings to my family, my dear friends near and far. I think of you even though the distance and the years are too far and too many. I have not forgotten my nearest and dearest. Those who have touched my life deeply and dearly. And to those who have come into my life with new energy, creative ideas that inspire and courage that brings hope when going through those tough times. We did it and did it with grace, dignity and thanks. For, those experiences open doors to enlightenment giving us the will to move forward. In unity. Together we make the impossible happen. When we believe and keep stalwart in mind, body and spirit. So once again, I will add, "This is dedicated to the ones I love." Know who you are. Take precious care.

Patti Z.

PREFACE

Memories come back to me. The time when I first noticed my little cottage house. Actually, it was the English Gardens that drew me in. For at the time, I was living in a beautiful Condo at Lake Point on the twentieth floor. Incredible views when looking out and down. But, too high to see the boughs of the trees or hear the whispering of the wind gently blowing through the leaves. I was safe and secure in my beautiful surroundings but I had just learned of the financial loss that would have serious consequences to my life, as well as many others. Leaving me with uncertainty about future security. And quality of life. I didn't want that to happen for there was no reason except greed that grew to out of control from those who changed the rules to suite them. The love of power and money became more important than the end result of their actions. Except there would be no end. For the rules were in their favor. They had control of their own destiny. Without a concern for others. I could never understand that mentality. Where was the voice of reason, concern or compassion? Were they invincible and so deserving now, because of all their daring in the successes so renowned?

I loved my beautiful place. I was fortunate. But, could I still afford to live there? How could I ever recover my loses, when there was no accountability any longer? I had to be sensible and not overreact. In the back of my mind, I knew I would eventually work it out. I'm driving to Sunnyside Gardens for a few plants that might work for my balcony. It was windy up there on the twentieth floor. That was the issue with being up so high in the sky. I'm driving down Abbott Ave. when I saw an open house sign. Ordinarily this would not have caught my attention. But it was a beautiful sunny day. And this quaint little house caught my eye. There was thick ivy climbing up the walls, the English gardens so bountiful and beautiful. So picturesque. There were river birch trees looming from behind the house with a huge pine tree in the front, the branches of pine needles practically touching the house. I was intrigued with all the possibilities. It was a small little cottage house. So affordable. The taxes would not be high. Such an inviting place. I could picture myself there.

I would stop in. But I couldn't stay for long for a friend was waiting at my condo. The real estate agent happened to know me from my previous house in Edina. Because she knew some of the history of my previous house, I felt I should tell her of my latest financial experience to let her know where I was coming from. I wasn't in any hurry to buy. Just started looking, gather information. I didn't see the entire house, just the main level. Things started happening quickly from here. Once I showed a certain amount of interest. I didn't realize this house had been on the market for over a year. Biding their time for the right buyer. It was way overpriced. I counter offered. Instead of 500,000 I would pay 470,000. I thought this house must be in perfect condition. The taxes would be lower. But I only had a month to move. Red flags all along to the end. Even though I knew this couple, through choir they would not be at the closing. Opening the door, opening the drawers, turning on the water faucets and more. Problems, problems greeted me at every turn. And unreachable.

I bought my house for way too much money and with numerous nondisclosed problems. No one to turn to. Avoidance, until the statute of limitations expired. They knew how to play the game. This would not have been so bad if my money had been safe. I thought it was. But now I was limited in what I could do to repair from its' broken state. How could I afford to do and be what was needed? It would take almost twelve years. Doing the repairs in increments of what I could afford. One thing I felt good about was paying on the principle all those years—a considerable sum for me. But I was determined to make up for the losses that I had encountered. Others would prosper. But I still felt there would be restitution one day. I noticed the changes in the housing market and real estate industry. Because, I was still recovering from my long illness, I was encouraged to move before selling. It would alleviate the stress for me and be easier for everyone. I could not understand that rationale. Yet, I knew I had to take care of myself. My health was too important to ignore.

My house was not sold yet but there was still some strong interest. I was told that the buying season was slowing down. The positive I could take my time. Move at my leisure. Toward the end of September, I had a buyer. I had met them. I liked them both. They were both professionals working downtown, wanting to be closer to the city. It was the commute thing. We had the closing. It was changed several times. Therese said I didn't have to be there. I told her, I had to be there. I didn't want any surprises. I wrote a note with the keys on a special key chain. They gave me a small box with a small ceramic bowl that I will treasure. I wanted this closing to begin with friendship and promise and end gracefully with dignity and consideration for everyone involved. It was not an easy winter. Spring and summer offered more rain and thunder than normal. I know we'll get through the worse when we work together.

Acknowledgement

Just writing this book has been an incredible journey in itself, with memories and feeling brought to surface, as further understanding and for closure too. This is my third book of this nature. Emerging from the experiences felt and learned in both my first and my second books. I felt this was the time of involvement and evolving. Seeing and experiencing the growing dysfunction and corruption insidiously growing, almost consumingly taking over what was once healthy and good. Feeling the heartache to heartbreak, the losses, the strong empathy. Yet, seeing and experiencing the effect of apathy, lack of consideration or concern. Not wanting to get involved or rock the boat for whatever reason. Maybe, from sheer curiosity or testing the waters to see how much one could take before the break. And the brokenness does appear, in many forms. But unaware that it comes from those who dare. Who are daring in their ventures that do impress those around wanting to emulate, be part and take part in the thrill of it all. Grandiose plans meant to impress but the grandeur wears thin and shallow. For there is nothing of substance to offer others. When we stop and look around and finally see the despair and the disparity. It is time that we start learning the truths from the rhetoric, distorted facts and address the hidden agenda for what they are. And bring to the table/forum something of true worth and value.

That is our family, our friends, neighbors, communities here, there and abroad. United in sincerity and purpose shared values that are lasting, heathy and good in mind, body and spirit. For this reason, I will include those who helped with the outcome and encouragement of my books. I was compelled to write my first. Even though in the beginning I rebelled against the computer. I

7

wrote free hand, pages and pages until too vast for pen and paper. Therefore, I need to acknowledge Jim Andrews for insisting I get a computer. We went to the Apple store and bought my first. To me it looked like R2D2. I didn't have a lesson. I should have. But I was so excited when I started writing seeing the transformation to be my first book. That was a magical day. So, thank you Jim and your partner Jim Bartingale. What a wonderful name. Time has passed, sometimes not so gently. You both brought incredible experiences not forgotten for priceless and precious to me. Eventually after so many pages, I realized I would need to get a publisher.

At the time, in early 2000 I chose from three—I liked the name Xlibris. Made a call and was introduced to Ronald Reese. Was he a movie star, I didn't know? Sounded like to me. It took me 9 years to write my first book. Learning in the process with lots of lost writings along the way. But Ronald Reese had patience, allowing me the time needed, to learn and grow. My life was filled with changes and distractions at the time. That is what took me so long. Also, I guess a little fear and trepidation. That proved unfounded. Thank you, God. This was also the time I was involved with the guardian ad litem program. I felt this was the time in my life that I could help others. Be a service, even an inspiration. I would have a family to help, guide, be a dependable and reliable person to turn too. This was actually a little more complicated and more to it then that, I would learn. My family was a mother and her two daughters Carol McGill and Stephany and Angela ten and nine years old. I met Charlene the foster mom too. We worked together to try and rebuild the experiences past into a better future. For this I want to acknowledge "you" overcoming the odds to start a new. Maybe one day we can have a reunion.

So, between writings, volunteering and learning my daughter would be getting married. Life was full and unpredictable. I would meet incredible people in this space of time Priscilla, Ida, and take-charge Julie and writer friend Linda Frazer. My dear friend Bernie Lindgren accomplished pianist, scholar with passion for life filled to the brim to the end. During this time, I also met Susan Lynn.

My artist friend who is now a mother to Tahlia. As I had written I met her through Gunnar. He was a burst of energy, enthusiasm brimming with plans and ideas. So, never a dull moment. He loved meeting new people. His circle grew including my friend Jill. Two Swedish entities and both strong personalities. My friend Pat Duffey such a zest for life, loves beautiful things, and interesting people. Generous with her time and presence and many times presents too. Tennis brought us together as well as our other endeavors inspiring each other through our conversations or our creative interests, and Cammy you're in this too, not enough time to do it all. My dear friend Red, who married a most warm, lovely woman of shared interests. Such a happy life now.

Now, since I mentioned tennis. I do have to recognize a few of my tennis compadres of all shapes and sizes, styles and abilities with always the love of the game. Grace Chung. Remember me? Us? My first tennis partner when we moved here to Minnesota. Until, you and your family moved out east. You found me a new tennis partner, that looked a lot like me. How did you do that? Ceil Stroik. What a team we were. Fun with lots of similarities, but differences too that complimented our game. Linda and Marcie Taylor were doubles partners on our team. Our lives have changed as well as our game. My Tuesday group at the Oakdale Club with Candace, Renee, Susan and our dear Madeline who moved back to Italy. She was our star. Then at the Flagship Club-- Carol Erickson, Barb McPhearson and sometimes Bob would sub (Barb's husband) He was fun to play with us, a gentleman and a rather crafty player. Almost all the Barb friends would play Barb Hauser, Barb Hagan and more Barbs. And, they all are pretty amazing players. Maybe, I'll change my name to Barb. Because, I was writing for so many years, most were aware. And they would sometimes offer advice, such as beware, be careful, tread softly. But, mostly interested and inspired to one day. They would have something to say.

I'm not quite finished. But almost. I have to mention Joe who is an avid player and attends the desk at Oakdale Tennis Club. Always has a smile, interesting and interested too. Outside of

9

tennis, there are many I need and want to acknowledge. Family and friends are such an entity in our life that enhances, renews our interests, enthusiasm and belief to carry on, amidst all the changes that rearranges us. I don't want to forget those precious moments in time. My friends / cousins Judy and John, Frank and Susie enduring and endearing through the worst of times and the best of times. I hope the worst is never more. Memories of B.J. Richards and Shelby Torrence when I was asked to be a scorekeeper, when 35 and over tournament from all over the states were held here in Minnesota at Northwest Racquet Club—before it became Lifetime Fitness and Tennis. It all wasn't a dream, but a memory that I want to hold on to. Is that possible? When we are all so scattered and our lives so busy. Time is now such a luxury. But memories are forever.

I would move when I was just finishing up my first book. I moved to my little cottage house. Where once again unsurmountable changes. Challenges so unexpected. I thought I was all done with that. I had paid my dues. What more would be expected. But, though it all, good people came into my life. My neighbors Sam and Paula, Bill and Rose, Wes and Dawn my neighbors next door. Now Art and Jeanne. They all have families. I would finish my first book. Because of the non-disclosure I wrote my second book. Selling my house, realizing everything I put in the house and outside too became a labor of love. That I did for myself and all of you, for this unique community. I wrote my second book in my little cottage house after completion of my first book. I received a call of interest from Dean Archers. He appreciated the intent of my first book. Through conversations and words encouragements I would work with Dean throughout the process. I had never heard of Book Whirl before, but Dean's enthusiasm and passion allowed me to trust. He is a good man, but the process has a different role. Working with Dean was uplifting but unfortunately the process was painful, for Dean and for myself. We live and learn. Dean I always wish you and your family well, for you are deserving for better.

When I moved from my little cottage house under extreme circumstances, I knew I was to gather my energy to write one more book, of this nature. So, a continuation of my first book and my second also. When the dust is settled and the cobwebs blown away—I will write my Art Book and some children's books. This will be lighter, brighter and a release, a pleasant change of pace, for me. But in this interim I had many conversations with Andy. Andy Sullivan, coming from a different perspective. Yet his enthusiasm, his passion and determination of my work was always evident. Giving me the impetus to continue even when tired and weary, even at times doubting myself. Thank you, Andy. It hasn't been easy jumping over all the hurdles and traversing through all the twists and turns of the unexpected. But any great endeavor never comes easily. Maybe it is a test for all of us.

I would like to add a few more names. Some from the past whom I've never forgotten and in their own way have offered me substance and reason. And, those in the present so meaningful and necessary in this time of life. Therefore, to Mas and Megumi Ennui and your precious children "now pretty much grown" Akeni and Soichi. We were your family when you came to Edina from Japan to stay for two years. That was a very special time and went way too quickly. Akeni was just a baby of three months. Mas and Megumi, your presence, your gentle humor and graciousness was exemplary. We haven't forgotten you. I think of you often, especially when leafing through the photos of that time. Take precious care and one day hope to see you once more.

Now, I will add a few names to the now, Karen and Bob Watson, Karen and Fred Walker you are extraordinary to me. Andrea, I feel we are kindred spirits, Debra Wyrobek, Debbie Vick and Scot Bohlsen all with busy lives but taking time when needed. I have to include Paul Kothrade and his wife Ginger working so hard to improve and repair. That is endless and takes dedication, determination and working together. The perfect team. Chris Rozzman another bright star and unforgettable. Of course, my sisters Marybelle, Ginny and in spirit our dear sister Sandy. We miss you. My brothers Rammy and Billy in Texas and their amazing and beautiful families. Now my own children Mark, Duane, and Monica

11

I love you so. You have given me gifts of grandchildren. Michael, Joseph, Melissa and Jenna. Michael married Therese and have a superstar baby Tony. Then there is Monica and Phil's children Lucia, Vince and Zoe. When I told them that I have finished my third book, they were in wonderment. What did you name your book Momé? What is the title? Well, I decided to title my book Bohemian Momé. They all laughed so heartedly. Then Lucia stops laughing. I like it. I like it Momé. Yes, we like it! Zoe then says, "we'll make it viral. Ah, I don't know if I want that. I don't want anyone to get sick. But, Momé that's a good thing. Spread the good word. I love my family, my friends so dear. May this book enlighten and inspire for the better.

A note: Danny Seipp did the photography for this book. I also worked with Linhoff Studio in Edina for the interior photos. Kim did the back-cover photo for Little Cottage House

I write for understanding, clarity, and truth.

To be known our reason and purpose.

Opening the door finding the pandora box to finally

release the secrets held too long and too deep.

Finding and discovery of facts and figures, numbers too.

The whole story is meant for you.

For then you can decide for your yourself what you choose.

Truth or dare, examining the cause and affect

chapter 1
OPEN DOOR

Right now, I am in a position too familiar once again. Yet, my surroundings are so different. I have moved from my little cottage house. I miss it so. The contrast is so great a difference. Am I prepared to accept this new way of living that could lull me into a complacency that I am not ready or willing to accept especially embrace? Yet, all the circumstances and turn of events prior to my move did necessitate all my decisions, including moving from my home that I grew to love. Was not easy at all…

For, whatever work I do is to be for a greater understanding and balanced life. For the betterment of society when acknowledged and knowing we all have capabilities that have not been recognized even within our own self. Within our self. And when we do have that revelation "our life becomes more meaningful and our purpose and goals more relevant, more worthwhile and to tell you the truth— more exciting." We are in this world together. We are united in purpose. We are family, friend, partners in this life. Let's make it work for all. Let's not be fragmented in the disconnect of this life. Let's build and bring together in unity and make it right. I think we can do that. Stand up and accomplish the seemingly impossible. Awareness and enlightenment is so important to teach and reach the potential that is meant to be.

Well you know, my life has not been easy. Challenges in almost every form—from early on. I knew I had to be aware of my senses. What was going on around me. Could I accept or was there an undercurrent of apprehension, a certain foreboding or warning. Sometimes, maybe a little more subtle as If was in the learning or growing stage or process of trusting my instincts. But yet, I also had that deep curiosity factor. So inquisitive. I wanted to know. I wanted to know, how and why. Especially, what is it that takes us so long to learn and understand. Why are there so many obstacles of every kind? Roadblocks and detours taking us on a most circuitous route. Leading us to an adventure or intrigue. Sometimes even a mishap throwing us off our course, taking up valuable time and exhausting our energy. Is it what we want to do? Is it where we want to be? So, life itself is not easy. That is why it is so important to be and try and stay healthy in mind, body and spirit. We need all our senses to traverse this life. It takes a long time to learn and that is why...

I'm still learning. For right now, I am in a position too familiar once again. That puts me at a dilemma not of my choosing. And, I pay the price. The longer I try to ignore—the quandary grows and continues to pull at me. How could this have happened to me—again. When will I learn? Now, what do I do? What can I do and how do I approach this rather delicate situation? As a giant puzzle too fragile to move. Too many parts. Too many pieces. I feel as I write all the possibilities will come together. I'll have a better understanding, a clear picture. The puzzle once scrambled and distorted now makes sense. A clear picture now on an intellectually sense, a ken of significance, now knowledge and understanding the reason and purpose of transactions processed to fulfill. Or be fulfilled to completion. Pull together and put together the perfect picture—the perfect package. But, is it faire and square? Or, is it loose and off balance—a little off kilter? Will this work or will someone be hurt? I don't want that—ever.

I've always believed, when we have experiences that are life changing or so profound that we can no longer ignore or accept—then we need to address. Not harbor those experiences in our subconscious to stew and simmer to the boiling point or become too hot to handle. Or, because of our precious pride. Aren't we infallible—a picture of virtue? We certainly are capable. Aren't we? For look at what we've accomplished and achieved in this life. Rewards and recognition. Trophies and plaques. Titles of value and titles of worth. Entitlements, special privileges that we all should

16

be so lucky. But the price really is too high. When we really look around and see what and who had been sacrificed or lost in their loftiness and grandiose schemes.

When our economy collapsed—instead of restitution to those who lost their homes, financial security and more became just another unfortunate casualty. Those who caused were rewarded. Instead of paying off their losses—the money was pocketed. They became wealthier than ever. Never gave back the funds or savings of others. They used to ensure their own purpose. They would for certain be financially secure. The majority of people who trusted and lost so much were in sudden shock, embarrassed for themselves to be found in this unexpected predicament. So bewildered by the turn of events they became immobile with shock. Still trusting or wanting to trust that their funds would eventually be returned. Many lost their homes to the banks or went bankrupt. Those who kept their homes—their taxes kept going up along with inflation. So financial struggles, deprivation, losing their quality of life now working harder and longer hours. At the mercy of those who kept it all with no returns. How could this have happened…

17

Knowing history, you would think we all would learn and not repeat those same mistakes. Put our trust in the vulgarity of actions so bold and daring seemed to impress into oblivion our common sense. Our own instincts squelched by the decisions made—borne out of our own fear from suppression and oppression becoming dependent on the meager crumbs dealt. Just enough to sustain, but not enough to restore and regain their value and their worth until the deprivation becomes so great that even the necessities in life have become unreachable, unaffordable and outsourced. Those who caused this disaster have removed themselves to the lofty comforts of their homes in gated communities surrounded by their peers and friends who think alike, talk alike, even need to act alike. And, whatever you do, don't question!

When I wrote about the necessities in this life now became unaffordable or nonexistent and how they were actually able to accomplish this brazen idea. Oh, they built their team from the most impressive and influential departments and compartments. Special laws and designer packages were written and given carte blanc to those who joined their faction. And it grew. And they transpired amongst themselves. They were guaranteed at this time not to fail. But, to complete their mission of impropriety with the help of their friends in high places and deep pockets. With each deceptive transaction proving its success, there also grew to be no boundaries. Nothing or no one to intervene or stop those nefarious actions would be become law, rule, commonplace and acceptable. New rules were made to make possible. New businesses were formed from the brokenness of the forgotten. Not borne of sincerity and desire to provide and restore growth with dignity. It was an allusion. Just busyness to keep the masses busy giving false hope, empty promises and impossible dreams. Life is not supposed to be like this…

18   Unfortunately, it wasn't just the banks and large corporations. Rules, limitations and restrictions were made that would affect the schools and education-what classes would be taught and how classes would be taught and which subjects would be eliminated. Even recess and school lunches deemed to be unnecessary. Who makes such rules cannot possibly have a child or understands the importance of having a break, a stretch, even some down time to talk and interact with classmates and teachers? Our schools should be a place of building blocks to your dreams, making it all possible starting with your ABC's and your 123's learning the alphabet for a child is so exciting. Learning to count and the learning of math from adding and subtracting, to multiplication and division. Oh, and that big jump to algebra to geometry once mastered, on to statistics, calculus and more.

Not everyone is into numbers, but the more you know lends you to more opportunities and abilities. Now, once the alphabet materializes and a child can read—I always say, "if you love to read there is nothing you can't learn." You can learn anything that interests you, and even conquer what is seemingly so difficult. And, that becomes really exciting! Books! Discovering the love of books to be read to learn, inform, educate. Reading at your own leisure to relax or bask—to take you to another place or time. You're never bored when having a good book at hand. There is a wealth of information in those pages of books of choice. Make it worthwhile. We retain more information reading a book than any other method. Well, going to good lecture certainly is wonderful. But, be sure to take notes. Therefore, be sure to write legibly. First, we learn to print, and then we learn to connect the letters to form a word. That is cursive or handwriting. I had a rather interesting experience. No, not interesting but rather surprising…

I was making a purchase and was told to have this clerk sign one of the forms. Hmm, that was interesting. But she quickly scribbled something. I felt bad for her, but curious also. So, when I saw her markings, I thought, "how sad," does she have a problem of some kind. So, I did ask her. She retorted, that she preferred not to write, that mark was her signature. All I'm thinking is—the dumbing of our country. I told her, "I didn't think that was such a good idea. When she represented the company she worked for—it wasn't dignified or appropriate. You give your best. It shows you are capable, qualified." She totally disregarded what I said. So, I decided not to do any business with that company. That was that. The main thing is…

That is one of the subjects or classes that have been eliminated in our schools. Not all. But, way too many. And, knowing how to write is a plus in life. So, if you find out that a certain subject is not being taught. Speak up for your child. That is a simple but necessary request. And, if they refuse, cursive is a great art to teach yourself and your child. Together, another bonding experience. And, the rewards will be so fulfilling. Talk about fulfilling and I must add inspiring is the importance of music, choir, glee club and art classes. Music relieves the tension that builds up. Music and the arts are somethings that we have in our life—as a gift. A gift to our self and to others too. When we are introduced to the arts in some form-- our life is enhanced and nourished while complimenting

19

our studies, work and play, our relaxation also. Offering a healthy diversion. Which we need in this busy, topsy turvy world. We achieve by learning, through our career and work of choice applying our creative gifts with blends of music, dance and the artistic world. And we all know the importance of sports, building team spirit. Being and staying healthy Is a must. Incorporating diversity into this educational time of life will prolong a positive and healthy experience. That is what we want we all want...

But isn't it rather interesting, probably more disturbing, frustrating even? The thing is when we ignore these supposedly small changes in life and we say nothing, do nothing not even question for some unknown reason. Maybe we are too busy and have enough on our plate of responsibility. Or no longer have the time or the inclination to go beyond this moment. Especially if we think that it's just immaterial a test or trial period of adjustment. Or maybe, testing the water to see if we were listening, care enough or understood the ramifications of these subtle changes that were (and still are) made hastily, without much thought or consideration. Is opening the door to the unfolding of serious consequences.

20

Before and after the collapse of our economy there became a subtle erosion of our conscience and consciousness. Using a formula through ratiocination--knowing data given in research of demography to further their grandiose plans or I should say schemes. For is it for the good of all or is it to impress or further their own best interest? Becoming a business venture of high stakes. determined to move forward at any cost. In the process throwing away the best part of themselves, their honor, integrity, and truthfulness. Common sense now long forgotten. Just driven, to even researching the topography of districts that would be suitable for a purpose of their own desire to acquire, take possession and do as they wish. Their real intentions kept in the dark, hidden until revealed and it's too late. Initially, there is a valid reason for these endeavors. But too many times will become ventures, reckless and daring, taking risks becoming not only costly but dangerous too. Seems we are more impressed with the wealth acquired than knowing the real intentions or motives. Will these actions be constructive or destructive? Time will tell. But, why do we wait so long when there are red flags all along.

I have been thinking and wondering what drives us. We are all so different. Our abilities and gifts are the center core of who we are and really can be quite extraordinary. Our personalities too. Unique. Maybe, a little eccentric or an enigma, mysterious and alluring or charismatic and the life of a party. Maybe quiet and demure, thoughtful and contemplative a late bloomer who finds his or her voice to be heard when introduced to their passion in life—a surprise to others, including themselves. Then of course, those who are bursting with energy letting their presence known. Eagerly waiting to spread their wings and fly, test their limits and reach their destination as soon as possible. We have "some of each" of those attributes, depending on what we've experienced in life, growing up, our teachers throughout school, who taught and inspired us and believed in us too. Our strengths and knowledge coming to fruition. Our interests heighten our passion and determination to our commitments and abilities that become our gifts for life. What we've learned will guide our way, our own path, in our own time in this journey of life. A strong foundation in life is so important. So, teach your children well for they grow up so fast. Yet, seems we aren't quite ready and never really prepared.

Regardless, we move forward in today's fast paced world. We are led to believe we make that decision—now. Otherwise we lose everything maybe our health, maybe even our wealth—or whatever meager allowances left to divvy up to all parties involved. We say a prayer for guidance and strength, wisdom too. We pray we're making the right choices, that our decision-making is of good judgments. But. It is a complicated world of information overload, excess of too many options but always an unexpected element or a loophole not understood that will surface after the deal is sealed. With the advancement of each technology learned—is promoted such possibilities of all kinds. We're excited to be part of this new world that our excitement overrides our good judgment and common sense. We want to believe. But we can't quite discern the murmuring voices going on around us. For it's too much to process when already on overload—sensory and physically. Combine it with a big disconnect, with values gone askew, integrity just another word that we all want to have within us. Or at least, we want to trust again. Surely, we all have learned our lessons including those at the top of the heap.

Something is still missing or lacking—a component that is essential for our existence and for the fulfillment of all life even our destiny is at stake. If we never admit that mistake or right that wrong. And, we just let it slide. Too tired. Too weary to process. Realizing, in the years that have passed—the roadblocks and all the treacherous curves. So many. That presented tremendous obstacle courses meant to keep us off balance. And, for way too long. Sometimes, never given a break. Weakening our resolve and our resistance. But we need to be alert more now than ever before. For we can't afford to lose any more or sink any lower. For, these transactions were made to profit, control and manipulate to their favor. There would be new ways to explore untargeted areas to ensure their funds would always be replenished. No longer (for now) would the stock market be used as before. Too many people were hurt in the economic crash-- never to recover. The devious minds were working overtime in the guise of impressive positions. Using the latest and greatest technology available to reach as many people as possible even if misleading. Didn't matter that it wasn't for the good of society. For revenue and profit was and is their impetus. How much more can we afford to lose? And, when is enough for those who love money and power more than…

Their sisters and brothers, and those around who put their trust and confidence in such people who have used and abused. They are only human too. All the money in the world is not going to make them any smarter, wiser, more loving and compassionate or honorable and trusting. God gave us all a gift of life. What we do with our gift is our gift to God. Why don't we make it good, lasting and beautiful? Instead of destructive and harmful-- provide the tools needed to uplift, teach and grow. That helps everyone. Including those who have forgotten. We continue learning in this life. That is the most wonderous and amazing gift we have. But we will lose it. If we misuse our gifts instead or appreciating and taking care and taking care of what is going on around us.

This is not a perfect world. But we still need to be aware of what is happening around us. Are we overworked, sleep deprived, indulging to the point of excess that affects our health, state of mind, or our bank account? Have we become so desperate that we compromise our integrity and those nearest and dearest? Let's not do that ever again. For we can rise above any situation when we take time to think and remember our reason and purpose and the consequences when left unchecked but worst when discovered. We must focus on restoring and providing instead of profiting from past mistakes and creating more problems through marketing sensationalism for profit. That is an erosion of our conscience and our sensibilities. We need to question—who profits from these endeavors? And to what degree will the losses be.

After the collapse, the government (big and small) opened the doors to new opportunities and opportunist too. Trying to regain the favor of the millions of people who were so adversely affected. Now this has been going on for many years. The erosion of our quality of life. We didn't complain that much. In fact, rather stoic. Finding the simpler life easier to bare than all the expenses leading to nowhere. No one to turn to for we have become the unreachable. Everyone has their own phone—another added expense. Yes, but we can text. And in the meantime, created another disconnect. We can watch movies and play games. Listen to music and do selfies in the dark and at the park. Oh, we can be reached anywhere provided we recharged and we know that new number. Or is it a scammer? Can't forget the GPS that will take us everywhere, sometimes to places we shouldn't dare. How wonderful that we can put our schedule and daytime planner on mobile device. We don't have to think anymore. Wakes us up and puts us to bed. Entertains us and drains us. Is it possible that we trust technology a bit too much? And

I don't mean just monetarily or momentarily. Hmm. Interesting combination of words. If we heard. Are we listening? Are we here in the moment or in a zone of no return? That is pretty scary to me.

I value my health. My mind. My spirituality. I want to be aware of what is going on around me. I want a fair playing field. I want to know the same rules apply to each and every one. But I'm uncertain that would be possible. Yet, I haven't given up, but we must realize we have gone off course. We are not centered any longer. We have gone too far to the left and some way too far to the right. We need to be centered. Not only in body but in mind. And we always need our spirituality as our guide. As we grow, experience and learn— our core being is strong. Not just physically, but all our senses. Mentally. Emotionally. Intellectually. Especially our spirituality are all connected. Helps to shape our character, our consciousness and wellbeing. We feel our best when we are centered. But when our energy is depleted or being drained by life's events-- we become vulnerable and in a weakened state. Then we need to refocus and regroup, meditate and reconnect. When we've gone way overboard, excessive for too long we become manic, delusional, and erratic. And, if gone too far will need professional help. Actually, in both cases. Too far to the left for too long, "I think of a catatonic state of being or of mind." Going too far to the right, I think of irrational, unapproachable, delusional and unstoppable, 'like jumping over a cliff to no return.

I thought as we evolved through life our senses would sharpen. For everyone. But instead, greed and desperation has taken over. Those who have it all always finds ways to more of everything. While those who have lost so much-- struggle to regain and recoup their losses. Pompous and pride pitted against humility and virtue. Good against the evils of the world. Who will prevail? Are we groomed and prepared to fill the roles and tasks or are we taking a leap of faith that we can get this right? Do we have the right team of shared goals, understanding and values? Or, is It a team thrown together haphazardly even thoughtlessly with misfits of various interests and abilities? Is the character ever questioned? Is this a cohesive team that can build unity instead of dividing and finding pleasure in the chaos? We have enough of that already. Therefore, it is important. If we stumble and fall or make that first mistake—is there someone knowledgeable who cares and knows enough-- to step in to correct and repair. Or, will they capitalize, manipulate and exploit to their advantage. And, who are to judge? Who is even capable in these times when our senses are dulled from excess or depleted from too much worry and too many debts? Created to profit one way or the other…

Before, we close on this note. Something to think about for you. For me and for everyone who will stop to think about this someday or one day. Awareness is so important as is so many other things that we take for granted. Life has changed dramatically in the twenty and thirty years. Leaps and bounds in every area, resulting in outsourcing and the elimination of products and structures that were comfortable and conforming, people friendly—easy to learn, easy to operate. But, after the economic crash in 2008, but (it started simmering and brewing long before that until) finally erupting and disrupting everything-- everywhere. Everyone was affected in some way or the other. We all remember. But, never really quite understood the whole thing. Just wanting to be done with and never repeat. Hmm. I'm not sure about that one. For, most people are oblivious and want to stay that way. Maybe, I'm wrong about that. I might be, "just tired and a bit overdone," But, I am still rather curious…

I wonder, through all the advancement of technology. The coming together of information from everywhere wanting to be connected. All in one. When we have all those census and surveys and important data and information of everyone recorded and documented for various reasons. What I am curious about is the status quo. There is a positive side of this technology what is needed to improve the quality of life. But there is a negative to every positive. When there is a negative that could lower or lessen the quality of life. We need to know the ramifications of those actions. For what and whose purpose and benefit. Is it a temporary inconvenience or will it impact future generations to come? How will it affect our physical health and wellbeing? Is this environmentally friendly or toxic to the land, waters or the air we breathe. Or even the way we think and feel? Is this still a safe place to live? Or, is this the testing grounds of things to come. Just a test you know. There will be some sacrifices. Enough, I say. Stop the madness. Stop letting big money, big government dictate the rules and outcome of our (desirable) communities. Stop making life so complicated and convoluted that you need a road map to reach every corner of the city or little desirable neighborhood.

chapter 2

GATHERING

I rediscovered my artist way writing journal. I had bought it in June of 1999. There were big changes happening in my life at the time. I had moved into the Calhoun Beach Club on the main level. My apartment was nothing special. But the views were exhilarating for when I walked out the doorway, was like having my own luxurious patio. Toward the center-- a meditation pond with water spilling over the infinity edge, cascading down the large boulders. On each side of the falling water were spiraling wide steps leading down to the restaurants, sidewalk cafes and to the beaches and lake activities across the street from me. This was everyone's favorite place to be. My senses were heightened. I felt alive, inspired and yet at peace. I belonged in this lovely place or space to reconnect with the part of me I had let go. Let be. Accept unconditionally. But I knew I could not completely. I would try and use this time wisely. I brought my piano. It fit. I had my new journal to put (pen to paper) my thoughts, ideas and chronicle the events and special moments in a very special space of time.

If I could I would have bought that apartment, but all these beautiful apartments were only for rent. Sure, you could rent for a lift time. But, was that practical? Renting these beautiful apartments in biking distance to the city served multiple purposes and catered to a specific demographic and professional needs. People moving out. People moving in. Very comfortable even luxurious accommodation for short term or long term with no real commitments and easy to relocate. I felt my healthiest in these surroundings of no pressure. It was here that I was introduced to Pilates. Keeping your center core. For me that made perfect sense. And, my instructor was precise. Yet, cautious. This was also during the time I was recovering from a tennis over use injury in my quads. I thought I would have to live the rest of my life with the pain. But doing Pilates strengthened the proper muscles becoming straight and strong once more. It was during this time I was encouraged to incorporate acupuncture to heal the tissues in my quads and around my knees. I was so thankful to be free of the pain. Move without fear and dance again.

Life is never perfect even back in June of 1999. For, as I am reading in my journal during that time—I could still feel the pain and anguish rushing at me once more. Why should I want to relive any of this? I do realize that the greater the distance sometimes we have a greater perspective and understanding. It saddens and surprises me too as I am reading, "I have not been in an environment to paint. For now, I am driven to write, trying to understand experiences that hurt me and held me back. For what reason and purpose, I could not convey? I am determined to move forward with dignity and grace." I would write, late in the evenings. Many times. For there would not be the interruptions that would occur during the day. Next page over, I wrote." I slept late this morning, after 8:30 am. That is new for me. But I feel I need that extra time to catch up. I've had late hours—3:00, 2:00 and 1:00 am. Last night, I was up until 12:30 am. So tired, I just crashed. Right now, I am outside my patio. It really is windy. My reflecting pond sprays the water high in the air. When I was watering the flowers—the spray from the pond misted my flowers and myself. It was refreshing. How lucky I am to be in such surroundings. It's not so bad to be alone here. And, an occasional an unexpected call or caller—to let me know I am not alone. Or should not be lonely."

As I re-read my writing from that time, I find it somewhat comforting. Yet, also surprised in the fact that even back then as harsh as the experience were, I never gave up hope. I fiercely believed that my words if heard or spoken would inspire and empower those who needed a voice of understanding to empower the people. Also, I wrote to awaken the conscience of those who forgot their real reason and purpose. I had written, back then, "So, I do know, power gone amuck can cause a lot of scars and tears. Where is the nurturing and respect for life and appreciation of beauty and talent? What causes some to be threatened by the virtues and abilities of others, that they would want to squash, oppress and suppress even destroy what is healthy and good. I am thankful that we have the talents of great artists, missionaries. Writers, teachers, doctors that continually go beyond to inspire—giving us hopes and dreams. Those who heal our bodies, our minds. May they always be. "I want to add, "We need our spirituality as our guide to keep us united in spirit, wisdom to guide us, courage to speak up, strength in our convictions and power to be heard and understood. Together in faith we are never alone. Always with Gratitude."

And, the next page over, that was June 24th. I had written. "I am adjusting. And, not just because it is a beautiful day. There is an appreciation and gratitude for what I do have, considering everything. I am still very fortunate. I had a busy but good day yesterday. My daughter Monica came over and we walked around the lake. Then we walked to Uptown, had a little light lunch and browsed the shops. I love being so close to my daughter." That was such a special time, I am glad that I included this is my journal. "In the afternoon, I did a little cleaning to prepare my windows here for my window treatments. I had fashioned from sheets and pretty fabrics I had and placed them on my windows. It was quite creative the way the sheets draped across the windows and was able to gently swag for an interesting effect. Very natural and rather bohemian. I felt good. I realized I could make do and be creative out of very little with interesting results.

29

I took a friend to the airport early this morning. Barb was so worried about making her flight on time that she wanted me to sleep over. I did. It was fun. It's nice and important to maintain and establish friendships. I played her piano, while Barb packed and did her organizing for her trip. We both are doing better than when our lives changed. So, dramatically. I guess, we both are pretty strong—our family has always been our main priority. It's good to see through that difficult time, we have made it. And, we will just keep moving forward, progressing.

It is now later in the evening. A musician friend of mine invited me to a Swing Band performance at the Wabash Street Cave. The music was lively and fun with many really good dancers. I mostly observed. But, during a break, Kim in traduced me to her trumpet partner. He was politely attentive. He asked me to dance. My life is complex. I'm not quite sure about the dating game, even now. I remember practically avoiding situations practically all my life—mainly, so I would not be noticed. Maybe, I really can't handle it. I don't know how. Do I play the waiting game? Or, I sometime take a chance and really let my life begin without interference or jealousy. How does one really know? Would be nice to take a couple of swing classes. Swing, going back in time. I wore my vintage sun dress, I bought for $8.00 dollars at Rag Stock. Amazing. I really like that little dress. You don't have to pay mega for nice things. I've learned that." I remember, it was a soft yellow, spaghetti strapped dress with a pattern of tiny flowers. Because it was so warm that day, it was the perfect dress, very feminine.

I remember that evening well as if I were there in that simple, pretty little dress. Not really the dress to do a fast swing dance in, but perfect for a beautiful and romantic slow dance. What was his name? I can't remember. Yet, I don't want to forget—the way he looked at me, when we danced. So, smooth. He was a gentleman. When I was to leave after the last break—he wanted to walk me to my car because, of the late hour. I remember how I felt, but how he felt also. Wanting to linger. Yet, I really did not know of this nice, handsome man. He did not know me, nothing of me. When we got to my car, he gently put his arms around me. Kissed me softly. But there was a sadness, a reluctance to leave but not possible to stay. Well, there is something magical and always romantic about music, ambiance and a warm, sultry evening. May we always appreciate these precious moments in time. And, maybe have a few more.

I am now at the last page of 1999 the 25th day of June. This is what I had written after the evening at the Wabash Street Cave known for their eclectic charm and electric ambiance. I drove there myself. Proud that I was able to find it. I didn't have a GPS either. I just did it. Oh, this wonderful place happens to be in Saint Paul. I am so glad they preserved this historic place. As, I preserved this memory…

I woke up early again this morning. I feel somewhat sad, alone. Was it the nostalgia of the music last night? Or the fact, that I am alone. Will I be able to trust again? And, if I am to give my heart, myself what are the consequences? Will it last and keep getting better, stronger a beautiful relationship. Is it possible in this world of discontent? Where people fear commitment or too tired. What is real? There seems to be game players as a business. Struggles. Time or financial or fragile state of mind. That is the world of a single person, who has been wounded. But, has survived. Now trying to pick up the pieces and find a niche in life, once more. Renew. Oh God, maybe I shouldn't write first thing in the morning. This is way too maudlin."

That is what I had written the morning after. It doesn't take long to recharge as I had written on my last page. "I've regrouped. Sitting outside by the reflecting pool. There is a gentle breeze that will be needed as it is supposed to be hot. But this is summer and that's okay for me. I'm wondering how I should use up this time wisely. As, this is a temporary space and eventually, I will have to do some serious house hunting. The thought makes me weary. When, I should be excited. It feels good right now, just feeling this breeze. I don't even feel that creative right now. I 've been looking for some papers that I need. I know, I had packed them with my important and immediate filings. They will show up—somewhere. The sky is so beautiful. So clear with wisps and puffs of clouds blowing through eventually gathering enough to form a different pattern. I am going to have to close and finish my projects. But, meanwhile, I hope this day brings a step closer to a normal life. The flowers I planted are so pretty."

31

That was the moment at Calhoun Beach Club. A brief respite from the storms. I wrote a little about the various flowers I had planted on that grand patio—a few perennials, of pinks and yellows with pretty blue flowers too. I even brought my concrete frog and filled him with wispy grasses, nestled in with delicate white and yellow tiny flowers, surrounded by the greens of the vines and leaves. I wanted to leave this place pretty for the next visitors.

Miniature Red Rose Nestled in the Boulevard Garden

One of the last flowers surprisingly are the miniature roses. As the summer days wind down. The nights get a little cooler. Sometimes much cooler. So, when we see the determination of this beautiful little creation defying the odds. It is a reminder we all can survive the storms. And the elements that can challenge. But, also the importance to be in your element to inspire

chapter 3

INSPIRATION IN UNEXPECTED PLACES

It was getting closer for my lease to expire. The more houses I looked at, the more foreboding I felt. I was also taking a course as a speaker for the protection of children. It wasn't until the last two classes, especially the last class. I would learn what a serious undertaking and how dangerous too. I didn't realize I was volunteering for a most serious program or mission. There needed to be a few more steps in this program instead of all those big bowls of candy at every meeting. What was that about? I wanted to work in the area of preventative. I wanted to talk to the families to inspire and teach and inspire a more conscientious, nurturing and loving way. Not hold them back with punishments that didn't quite fit the crime or the time. But that was never mentioned. I wasn't the worldliest or have the most formidable presence. I wasn't even that big. I did play a lot of tennis, but I don't think tennis would prepare me against this wayward, pervasive or perverse society. Instead of feeling capable I felt I was to crumble and grumble. Maybe a tantrum would work. Once again, I was out of my element What was I getting myself into? When I wasn't prepared to have authority over anyone or the outcome. When these cases seemed to grow out of control with very little help or desire for successful independence.

I always question when there are more problems than solutions. First and foremost, every child and adult needs to be educated to the best of their ability. Get to the root of the problems—remove the offender and protect the offended. I never felt that these programs were really set up to help the people in need. But keeping them in the system. For the more people in the system, meant more funding from the big government. Many people don't know this. Why do I find that so abhorrent? Once in the system so tight, almost impossible to be out of sight or out by life. I was able to save the family I represented. But it really was standing up against a broken system, with lots of determination and lots of documentation. Plus, I was a volunteer. There was nothing for me to lose. I have always believed in preventative. But what I could see happening was oppression and suppression. You can always find those whose main goal in life is to have power. Especially power over others. I want to see people thrive, achieve their goals and have expectations that is possible to reach when given opportunities. A little encouragement goes a long way and sometimes a helping hand in the process.

I learned I was the one who was given the most complicated case. I certainly wasn't expecting that. But I do have to tell you. I did meet them. Circumstances bring to the knees, humbled with no direction. I met this family, the foster mom and two sisters. They referred to the foster mom as grandma. Two young girls. They were ten and eleven. The mom was incarcerated. I know that word now. It's not what I thought it was. The whole thing. The entire experience inside and out. I worked with this family for over two years. They counted on me to help them through this time. I was determined to understand how the system could continue to fail and be part of the falling through the cracks. When the system itself was meant to hold and scold but not really in any hurry to release to independence. We don't ever want to be a state or country that instills fear and oppresses and suppresses our own people. There is a better way. The weak and inflated ego can do a lot of damage to others. We can't have that. We can't allow that either. God gave us compassion, wisdom and courage. All we have to do is ask and we will receive what we need. He knows. But a broken heart or mind is incapable.

chapter 4
LOST AND FOUND

Now, because I had this experience working as a volunteer (guardian ad litem) affected my decision in buying a house. I had never before felt this vulnerable. I wasn't afraid of the people who were in the system, but somewhat fearful of those who lurked within. That is when Peggy suggested I look at Lake Point. At that time, a condo to me seemed too removed from life. Maybe a little too secure, certainly very comfortable. Maybe even too comfortable but unaware. I looked at a couple of units, but when I saw #2004, I was drawn to the way the light fell into the room. I loved the entry way, the way the beautiful terracotta tiled floor led to a little powder room, turned the corner and into an inviting kitchen, leading into an eating area. The large windows on two sides of the room, the opposite wall was bricked with an opening into a library/den. I loved the graciousness and ambiance. I could live here. I remembered that the money I received after selling my house, was not at my bank. Tom Drees of Merrill Lynch told me I would earn a higher interest rate if I gave the funds to him instead of my bank I had used for many years. U.S. Bank and I had an alliance of sort. So, an interesting history. But it didn't appear my best interest was necessarily shared with this corporate bank. Tom D. assured me the sale of my house money would be secure plus 7% more. I knew I could afford these beautiful accommodations. This would be a birthday present for me. I called Tom Drees and told him of my plans. My decision. I gave him the information needed for Lake Point. He told me. "Everything will be taken care of. Congratulations."

I would be moving once more. From Calhoun Beach Club to Lake Point. It was a tall circular brick building. Built to accommodate the views from all directions. There are four lakes, sunsets of suburbia or western view and the sunrise in the east to the city—spectacular views in surround. When I bought #2004 the view from my living room and balcony was Lake Calhoun with parts of Minneapolis. From my office I could see the storms coming in and sunsets. From the casual eating area there was western view Cedar Lake, bike trails to the city. From the den, guest bedroom and the master bedroom overlooked Dean Parkway and parts of Lake of the Isles. Well, I could go on about the wonders of this area. That is what I fell in love with, the beauty, the vibrancy and so much variety and things to do. I was fortunate to have the opportunity to live at the beach club and the Ivory Towers as some of my friends would call my place at Lake Point. Lake Calhoun was just cross the parkway from Lake Point. So, it was close. If I had the time, energy and enough friends to move my furnishings—I could have done it myself. With lots of help. But that wasn't going to happen for I had a little bit too much, plus my piano. Changes happened quickly. I was thankful. I wanted to give back in some way.

I became very involved with various volunteer programs. Guardian Ad Litem program was the most extensive and definitely very serious. On call day and night. Since, I was a volunteer, I was also available on every holiday. Not only did I want to make a difference, I felt I could save the world. All, I had to do was show my passion. Enlighten and inspire. Teach and preach, I would be their advocate and they would achieve their dreams. They would reach for the stars. And, they would see the light. It all seemed so simple. But there were so many road blocks and obstacles set in place. For whose purpose? Were they there to repair? Or to entrap and snare. Once I was assigned my family, communication was rare. Sometimes, not given the right information. I felt like an investigator. My credentials kept expanding but for what worth I would never know. For they really didn't want answers. They liked those problems. I was the wrong person for this job. I focus on preventative and find solutions. There were solutions but they just didn't want to hear.

Stephanie, Me and Angela

I had just moved to Lake Point. It was beautiful. I felt removed from the difficulties and the traumas of my experiences. I felt I was now in a safe place almost as a sanctuary. In my gratitude I wanted to give back, to help families reunite, if possible. I heard of the Guarding Ad Litem program and was intrigued. Maybe this would be my direction to help others. I decided to serve as a volunteer and would attend programs for two month or so, along with those who were established in their profession and some who were studying law. This program would further their own understanding of what is needed. Seemed once again, I stood apart but coming from a different perspective I could offer valuable insights. We all want our intentions to be pure. Not influenced by experiences not understood or positions that once impressed but now have become buried beneath the pretense or rhetoric. Becoming an agenda not quite realized yet. But a steppingstone none the less. Leading to the field of their desire.

I would be given the awesome responsibility of reuniting a single mother and her two young daughters age nine and ten. At the time the girls were living with a foster mom, Charlene. I had changed the girls name and their mother's name also when I wrote my first book. For I wanted to protect them. Shield them from the past. For I knew their lives would be changing and I didn't want past regrets or obstacles to influence their journey in life. But I realized. They had nothing to be ashamed of in fact their love for each other was always evident from the first time I was able to observe their genuine love and concern for each other. They had tremendous obstacles set in place. And they would defy the odds. Which was never easy. But they had each other. Being together was their impetus, reason and purpose to achieve their goals. To rise above it all to inspire their dreams. For this reason, I am enclosing your names as a tribute and acknowledgment to Stephanie, Angela and your mom Carol. One day, when the time is right you can tell your own story. Document your own experiences. For understanding the reasons in this life that sometimes will also give us our purpose.

Here I am, ready to savor and enjoy my Ivory Tower. I felt like a princess or an elegant lady of leisure to be pampered and spoiled. Just a little bit. I don't think I ever had that luxury. For one thing, my friend Jim and I went car shopping. I bought the first one I saw, under the spotlight in the showroom. I never knew buying a car could be so much fun. "This is the one. Can I buy this one?" My fervor was spilling over. I had never bought my own car before. It sparkled like a diamond, except it was pearl white with lush black real leather seats. Heated too, for the long Minnesota winters. Well, my new car was perfect for my new luxurious surroundings. I'm thinking of this now. That was also when I was working as a Guardian Ad Litem. That was my only car. When I went to court for the girls or take them grocery shopping—I did that sometimes too, I would drive them to their programs, meetings even to see their mother when she was incarcerated, in my new shiny car. I never even thought of that before. Maybe, that was the reason—I stood out. I stood apart. I was different. Yet, I cared enough to take that beautiful car to the worse part of the city. But I know my own guardian angel was watching over me every mile. And, with a smile. Carol and the girls' needed groceries. We went to the store and I let them select what they liked or needed. I wanted them to feel comfortable for maybe one day, this could be their life. By the time we got the groceries in the trunk of the car, it was dark. It was a perfect winter evening. There were piles of the softest snow that just kept blowing from the streets and the skies. Carol and her girls were genuinely happy. Laughing as I'm traversing these streets for the first time. Assuring me and telling me what a great driver I was.

I breathed a sigh of relief as we emptied the trunk of all the groceries and Carol and the girls were safely back in their temporary home. All was copacetic. I'm driving slowly. As I look at my rearview mirror, I thought, "Wow, that snow really is coming down. I stopped at the corner stop light, and this big man is waving his arms at me. Saying something, I could not quite understand. The light was still red. He tapped on my window and said, "Your trunk is open. You don't want to get more snow in your trunk. I can shut it for you." He was a stranger. Concerned. I had no idea. I thought it was the snow stuck to my new car. I was so thankful. This was just another introduction to my new experiences. This was a rough neighborhood, but I never felt that…

I didn't just get a new car, earlier that day Jim and I went to buy my first computer. I was writing and I would read excerpts to Jim. He encouraged me and was never shy about telling me, "Patti, you really have a lot of run on sentences." He gently laughs. "Well, I've got a lot to say and I don't want to take time to put all those commas and periods or even add the paragraphs too, sometimes. I can work that out later. It's more about the content. The message you know." I cleverly tell him. Jim knew I had something of importance to say. I knew of my experiences not yet out there. He could see my experiences as a book. He wanted to take me to the Apple Store, so that's where we went. I came home with the cutest computer. It looked like R2D2 from outer space. He was translucent green with white. He would look great at my office desk. Jim set my new computer up for he was an expert. He set it up, so when I walked in my office it would speak to me. "Good Morning," in a rather sultry voice which always startled me. Jim gave me a few pointers and offered to help me anytime. Goodbye pen and paper. My writing was starting to look and feel like a book. Thank you, Jim.

39

I still like my paper and I'm a collector of pens and pencils. Erasers too. Markers of all kinds. And, do you know? Calligraphy is coming back. The art of writing. Computers. Pens and paper. We can enjoy both. It doesn't mean we have to do away with the tried and true. We can appreciate and value both worlds. Learn from each.

Right now, it's the morning of the 4th day of July—Independence Day. From a distance, I hear the sound of trumpets, the beat of drums. I open the sliding doors and step onto my balcony, I am drawn to the rhythmic sounds as I stretch and playfully march in step to the beat of the drums. I stop as I hear the high pitch of a fife, joining in perfect timing playing their part in the music of the

John Phillips Sousa Marches. How lucky I am to be so close—and yet so far but not removed.

Not sure if all the festivities will happen for the sky is grey and clouds rolling in. But, the perfect day to write. But, went to take a small break and the power went out. Evidently, there was a power surge. For over two hours without electricity, TV or radio. I was told not to open the refrigerator to preserve the food. The worst part was I felt I was stuck for my computer went down with everything else. The lack of power affected everything, including the elevator and the garage door. I talked to a few of my neighbors and relaxed for a short while on my balcony. The cloud rolling in brought a deluge of rain to add to the abundance of enough rain already. Explains the high humidity and the uncontrollable curl of my hair. But the electricity did come back on, just as they said it would. I want to add-- this is the year 2019 and Independence Day…

40

And this is what I had written in my (lost and found) Artist Way Journal-- Sunday the 21rst of February 2016. Wow, I found my journal (that will prove to be so valuable). The years have gone by. Not enough time to process even to heal from all the changes some unexpected but some made more difficult than need be. It seemed the moral compass was lost, broken or forgotten along the way. When I found this journal, I had just started working on a painting of a lion. Years ago, I had painted a magnificent head of a lion. I didn't want to sell it. But, was offered a price that he felt was so worthy. I was impressed by this offer. I reluctantly accepted. I often would think of this painting. For, he was grand. The lions' mane was thick and lush. I used a palette knife and various shades of yellow ochers and rusty shades to add to the rich golden and glorious oils to achieve the effect that I desired. I had that magical block of time and incentives also.

My friend Bob and I went to the Chicago Zoo. I saw this lion in the distance roaming the grounds. We stopped to watch. Then the lion stopped and rested his paws on this large plateau as if observing us. I took his picture through the chain linked fence. One day, I would paint him. Or try to, for years had passed with interruptions and disruptions. Not the best environment for an artist's mind or a creative mind. After finally finishing this new lion, people wanted to name him. He was not the same lion I had painted years before. In fact, he looked like a grown baby lion. Gentle eyes, and beautiful mane. His name would be Leo, Cleo or Cecil after the majestic lion who was slain by a trophy hunter in Africa. It was on the news, the papers, magazines too. Cecil happened to be the longest living lion in that territory. But, now no more. The trophy hunter happened to be a dentist from Minnesota. What is it about this state that seems to bring out the need, a desire, to conquer or control even to destroy? Is it for their inflated or frail ego or for the prize to impress or simply because the price or sacrifice is acceptable? Entitled once more. So many were outraged. Rightfully so. But the laws seem to protect the mercenary, freedom of speech, freedom of will but without boundaries or decency. It is amazing how we are so slow to learn or maybe too fearful to recognize when out of control or loss of our own moral code.

41

That was the first paragraph I had written in my journal in February of 2016. I started this journal in June of 1999 after many interruptions and years of lapses. I had lived for a short while at Calhoun Beach Club, then to Lake Point. I would live there for over six years. And then bought a little cottage house in October of 2006. I finished my first book The Value of A homemaker after I moved into my little cottage house. And my second book while in my little Cottage House amidst tremendous angst, lots of dust and constant construction. The world seemed to be coming apart at the seams, falling apart, value eschewed, desperation seeped in and then flooded the gates—in almost every area and seemed to bring out the worst in their desperate attempts to save whatever was lost in the fray of these times.

I wrote both my books for understanding, the heart of the matter. To empower those who were caught in the web of deception. My purpose was also to inspire to go beyond and rise above. Not give up. And, never be afraid to question. I try or tried to awaken the consciousness of those who caused so many hardships, heartaches, headaches and heart breaks to so many. Not to mention the ongoing stress of it all. For whose pleasure? Don't tell me it's for the revenue. Or for the love of money to buy their power over others. We've had enough of that. It doesn't look good or feel good for anyone. It only brings out the worst. We can and must do and be better than that.

Oh, I ended up naming my lion Judah.

In the second paragraph of that page, brought back the memory of doing my first art exhibit in South Bend, Indiana. That was also when I sold my first lion, plus two portraitures. It's not easy letting go even when the price is right. The interesting part of this exhibit was meeting and talking to various artist about their artistic life— their style, how they got their inspiration. During my last break, as I was strolling through the exhibit, I noticed this man painting on his canvas. He was standing at his easel painting in a flurry of broad, sweeping brush strokes. He was deep in his thoughts, captivated by the subject as if transported to another place.

42

As he is painting so intently, I quietly study his works on display. So interesting, his brush strokes bold, the colors dramatic, very prolific as on a quest to touch the soul of his work. As I watched this man, I felt his life was not easy. There was also a sadness about him. I felt, "His love of painting was also his healing." His work had a powerful energy that you could feel. His style was unique, his own, expressive. Not to impress, but to release his strong emotions. "Your paintings are beautiful" I told this man.

He stopped his painting to look at me. I hoped I hadn't interrupted him. I just wanted him to know of his talents in appreciation and encouragement. I didn't know. I could not tell if he was older or young. For I was young and naïve. And, anyone with whiskers seemed old to me. He appreciated my comments. Sometimes, my inquiries have no boundaries. But my intentions are sincere. I asked where he studied and where he got his inspiration. Then he told me, he used to drink—too much. Drugs too. He was on a downward spiral and got into a lot of trouble. He was incarcerated. I didn't know what that meant.

When he explained, I felt somewhat embarrassed and a bit bewildered. But he told me during this time of incarceration he was introduced to painting. "He discovered his love of art and his ability to paint. That became his salvation, his saving grace. His artistic world won out, over the bottle. He conquered his fears, overcame his weakness and found his reason and purpose in his powerful works of art. But it had to take his fall to find his strength in his creative endeavors. When he told me his history, I was thankful for I had a further understanding. I learned once more, "the healing powers of our gifts when recognized can do wonderous work and give inspiration to others also."

I think of the many people who have never had the opportunity, time, or encouragement to pursue their real interests, passion or explore the depth of their abilities that could be incorporated in their life to enhance even their work. I always feel to go beyond, test your curiosity if it's healthy. You never know what hidden talents that have not been tapped that could open doors of opportunities and new capabilities. Expanding all kinds of possibilities. That is exciting for everyone. And, everyone has that gift. We just have to look and sometimes go on a search to discover what we have lost or forgotten in all the hype of this life.

February 23, 2016, I must have had enough for I had written. Shouldn't life after many years offer a certain reprieve, some much earned leisure instead of a barrage of financial assaults? This is an ugly time (and I don't like that word) in our own history, our own country and worldwide. There is a huge financial disparity—that has been allowed to happen. Only a select few have controlled their outcome and income—at the cost of and sacrifice of others. We have become a society of disconnect.

44

"We must have had a good match, for we're still smiling."

Which made and makes it easy for those who benefitted through their privileges, entitlement, given every advantage with loopholes and impressive packages to make it possible. Exempt from moral behavior, without a conscience. When there is a disconnect, walls of silence, walls of avoidance set in place to achieve their outcome. Now privileged and deserving. I've written two books about this and it practically broke me, financially and emotionally. Again, my experiences were too vast, too many to be ignored. I had to write. To be silent would only perpetuate the madness, the dysfunction and corruption. I've had enough. And, as I look around see, hear and feel—we all have.

My intentions are in the right place. But seems never to have that consistent block of time. I want to crescendo into my day. But my days are long and too many times comes with a jump start. For instance, today was on going without a break. Until, I realized I didn't know if I was sick or just plain exhausted. I am going to try to see Dr Hu this or next week. (my acupuncturist.) I had written in this section of my journal, about shadow artist, gravitating toward the light, to their strength and their desires. They are (or we are) gravitating toward a better life, a better way—a place of peace, beauty and acceptance. But, should we accept certain behavior, conditions or injustice. Oh, that is such a big word. One that provokes all kinds of feelings. But, should be discussed until understood.

There is nothing wrong having ambition. Everyone is ambitious to some degree. But it is when a metamorphose becomes so startling a change in behavior or demands that is no long healthy, logical but for hidden agendas meant to control the outcome. Sometimes we need to step back, regroup, reevaluate our purpose. We need to check to see if we are still balanced / centered or coming off kilter. And, not just a person or certain people, but the company we work for, organizations and institutions, governmental, clerical to the clergy, to the top of the summit to the lowest valley. More times than not, we need to re-evaluate.

This was written the 25th day of 2016. Went to tennis today. Just the three of us Renee, Susan and myself. We decided to play Canadian doubles—rotating sides. When you were on the singles side, you could hit to the doubles court. But after rotating, when you had a partner, like in regular doubles you had to hit to the singles court. I liked that format. But not everyone liked to keep the score. I didn't mind, I could keep track of everyone's score. After each game, I would announce the score of each. That takes a certain amount of concentration. Sometimes they liked that idea, depending on their stress level that day.

This was a fun group, nice people and good play. But, through the years our lives have become more demanding, coming or going, catching up, trying to catch a breath or a moment of reprieve or reflection. For me there always seemed to be a sense of urgency to each day. I stopped to talk to Joe at the desk who worked at that little tennis club. At one point, I told him, "maybe, one day, I will write a book "Tired of this frenetic life." But then I added, "but I won't, for who in the world would want to read about someone's frantic life?" Joe laughed and said, "probably more than you think. Everyone's life seems to be frantic now a days." I didn't know if I should laugh or cry. And, what about the birth right? What does that mean? Are we born into a certain standard or class.as if from eons ago? Is our birth right what we are born to naturally? Our gifts to be appreciated, encouraged and groomed to perfection. Or at least, to praise, admire to inspire dreams to come, or reaching a stature in this life. When I returned home from tennis, I had a call from Victims of Torture agency. Occasionally, I give when I can. I never knew that torture was so common still prevalent in these times.

I heard of this organization after my divorce. Haven't we become more aware, more compassionate. But, wait! No, we haven't. Seems we are more disconnected and self-absorbed than ever—for preservation maybe. "of course, I will give. But we had that discussion once before., about emotional, psychological and physical torture." Some wounds you can see, even when you don't want to. The wounds that are buried deep for years will surface. When you don't see or feel the pain inflicted, the tears that are held back, the truths unspoken will come to light. For once again, self-preservation needing to kick in. Wanting to forget. Not remember. Not to see. Not to feel. Please, no reminders. But we can never forget. We cannot continually repeat those same mistakes.

I will continue using my journal to keep in order the series of events that would lead up to the actual sell of my little cottage house. This would be the writing on the 26th day of February. Some things we take for granted, our basic needs, our inherent rights. We rush through the day. Our intentions to accomplish everything in one day. Sometimes, we have that five star day, when things fall in place, smooth and orderly. Then we get a call or have a fall that pushes are routine or schedule into another slot. What is our priority? The importance from necessity or for the control of our destiny. Whatever, we will have to take a little more time, a little more care, pay attention to whatever is going on around us. Within us too. 47

Many times, we take on too many man- made problems and make them larger than they are. The worry, fear of the unknown, all the uncertainties pull at us. Are we able to do this painting, drawing or learn this piece of music, or learn to dance to the rhythm of life? We worry and think about it until it becomes larger than it really is. When uncertain, take baby steps or piece by piece as if a puzzle—a little at a time until complete. Enjoy the process. Most things do not need to be completed "right now." That again, is a man-made problem meant to control or profit in some way. When we live like that, "under a control" that is constant, eventually affects our quality of life. Do we or can we have quality work of art or present a quality project or ever have a quality life.

If the control is too tight and the price is not right or too high to attain what we love in this life. Even what we do in this life, we want to savor the moment, enjoying the process to create, or soak in the atmosphere of inspiration—a healing space, a healing place. For when we are rushed and feel are time is crushed becoming an impossible task instead of joy in the moment or satisfaction in our work or project—becomes a little shaky, shadowy, with thoughts of doubt? What have I left out? Where could I have done better? Question always. Maybe that is part of the process. Especially in these times. But whatever we do, even in those monumental distractions or interactions we need to take time and to be given the time to understand the importance of doing it right, making the correction and having the right connections.

Realize the importance of what we do lies in the finished project or transaction. Have we created a masterpiece, a fine work of art to be displayed to enhance and enjoy? But, it's not just about our artistic or creative life or world. It's also how we accomplish our goals, solve the problems—for ourselves and in leadership in all areas of life. I've said a creative or artistic person will find a healthy way to find and solve issues and problems in a healthy and honorable way. They will bring beauty, peace, purpose and inspiration without violence or destruction. It is the ability to convey through their work, ideas and shared experiences for understanding. Healing the wounds of doubt and fear. Embracing inspiration for the good of all.

This was taken from excerpts written the 27th of February 2016. This journal offered a small quote on each page. Meant initially for artist. I used it as that, but noticed it also applied to life itself, our work, our interactions and our reactions and tolerances throughout our lifetime. This to me was rather interesting. I had written, I believe we have had enough abuse in this life—to abase our self or anyone in the early efforts of development will stifle the creative growth. When these are gifts are to be explored and evaluated with appreciation, awareness and gratitude. I've found many times the process of learning, achieving and accomplishing our goals is the most exciting part. When you feel you've reached the pinnacle of knowledge or ability. Maybe, is the time to teach or mentor. Be that person that encourages the next rising star. Or, anyone needing a little boost of encouragement through time spent a few learned tips can be valuable, a little instruction and checking in every so often to see the progress or critique constructively. I love seeing progress, success in the making, another rising, shiny star. All unique with their own style.

Yesterday was fragmented with too many distractions. Until I realized I had to stop and take time for me. I made an appointment to see Mi Shawn and Renee—I would take a small block of time to be pampered, fluffed and buffed and put back together at the Beauty Room. Apropos for Mi Shawn so beautiful with the ability to bring out the beauty or the best in her clients as well as her staff. Renee happened to cut my hair that day. She had just finished writing her first book. She gave me a signed copy of hers. I had given her a signed copy of both my books. We had some great conversations about life, and the importance of doing what you love to do. She was a free spirit. Our lives were so different. Yet, complimented. Just seeing Mi Shawn gave me the added boost to my day—graciously.

When I got home, I had a meeting that was somewhat disconcerting. The strange thing is, from the time I just moved into my little cottage house, people would call or send a mailing with interest to sell my house. I just moved here. I learned that there was a tremendous amount of work that needed to be done. The offer would have to be well worth it for me to turn around and sell my house. I will never understand how realtors approached their work so fervently. As a competition or to achieve another sell in these desperate times. The challenge of it all or curiosity. But, really, now a numbers game. I want to stay in the moment, at least try and make it work. Which has not been an easy thing to do for we live in a time of disconnect and unspoken agendas. There has got to be a better way. One that has some thought and consideration, dignity and real purpose that is known and works for both parties. Other than the bottom line as the main objective and their incentive. Meanwhile, I'll continue working on my lion—Leo, Cleo, Cecil, or is he King. How about Kingston? Lots of possibilities.

Looking in the Window

There are giant ferns and lilies against the garage and the flower box with the sweet pea flower bursting forth in its' sweet simplicity. This was another surprise and inspiration for me. Simple elegance. Natural grace and wonder. The ferns on that side of the garage were especially lush and hearty. So much so, they would have to be thinned. I put steppingstones to lead to the flower box. To make it less of a jungle. Nature has a way to make its' gardens grow. Splendor in the grasses, ferns and a plethora of blossoms for evermore. But, looking in the window I see the reflection vaguely in the background. And, I do believe I see a horse. Is that possible? From a distance.

chapter 5
LEAP OF FAITH

February 28th 2016 I had written. Do we sometimes get caught up in the drama and all the challenges that have become a constant part of this life? Becoming normal for us. No matter how painful or frantic we can't get off the treadmill—even though numb from shock and uncertainty–about our circumstances our future. Because for so long this has been our life. What we have known. What we have lost but can no longer accept. My son Mark, his faith or his search of, has always been his quest. Search for higher knowledge, higher standards within himself. Yet, always testing himself and others too. His search is intense. My faith is within myself, a deep feeling and knowing that goes beyond my experiences. Giving me peace when I need, strength in my convictions and courage to continue for I know there is a reason and purpose in our experiences. To teach us. Test us too. But, always knowing we are never alone. That gives me strength in knowing my purpose and desire to do and be better. Not just for myself, but for others too. Just knowing there is a better way. Mark wants me to join the Greek Orthodox Church. His words when he called, reflecting on his profound experience in his conversion. He told me several times, "Mom, don't deny yourself." He wants me to be happy. Fulfilled in my faith. Life is complex.

The last paragraph I had written on that page resonated within me. What is needed yet, not always evident. I had written," I think that it is the worst—not caring enough to be bothered—not wanting to know just to control. Through it all, it was a step forward. But I wonder if it is possible in our lifetime, when it is too late in the land of disgrace. For fear that the truths be known."

Looking Out the Window

One beautiful summer day at my little cottage house, as I was picking up, "organizing somewhat" my garage that was filled with character and charm. I would look around in amazement and wonder at the construction of this garage well over a hundred years old. And, the fact there was a green door on the back wall that led to a horse's quarter. Off to the side are two double doors that led to the feeding area with bales of straw on the side. The straw strewn on the floor of earth, with bins of oats and apples as a treat to eat and nourish. Back then, many years ago there were fields of grasses to graze with plots of land for gardens. Just a smattering of houses nestled between Lake Calhoun and Lake Harriet. Life was simple, the air fresh and the water pure. That was way back then. This is now.

I Brush the cobwebs off the trusses and notice the light coming from the window. I feel inspired once more as I remove the cobwebs from around the window and clean the window to almost, sparkle. I see the sweet pea plant that has grown from the flower box. Where my friend Bob would put a few seeds in. With a hope and a prayer and a certain amount of loving care. A wonderful surprise. What would appear as I look out my window from the inside of my garage? Looking out that window. I went outside to see how the fragile looking little flower appeared from the outside. Equally inspiring.

chapter 6
ACCEPTANCE

Sometimes we have to take a leap of faith, especially since this is a the 29th day of February and a leap year. And, it's a Monday packed to the brim and overflowing. Even though we have added another day to catch up, it's still not enough. But I do like the concept of the leap year. I'm not a hairdresser, but my friend in her plight in this life comes over and likes me to cut her hair. Jill tells me, I think sincerely, "I don't know anyone who can cut my hair the way you do, Patti." Well that is for sure." I'm thinking. But then again, I do likes cutting hair. It's relaxing and creative and provides a service for I don't charge. I feel like a therapist and a hairstylist at the same time. I even have haircutting scissors and various clips and combs to pull hair up or back. My friend talks, I listen and concentrate on giving Jill the style of her desire.

Depending on the weather, I will cut her hair on the back porch or the side porch. But since it was still cold. We set up shop near my piano and dining room table. It was a nice way to catch up and practice new skills at the same time. When we clean up, Jill likes to gently sweep up her golden locks of hair (almost white) and give her hair clippings to nature, for the birds to build their nests. Jill loves her baby soft flaxen hair and so do the birds. They think of these golden threads as a treasure, making a most luxurious nest. And it is and it does.

That is one of the wonders of life, to be flexible, capable, and accommodating, I will always try new things, sometimes with a little fear and trepidation. But, if I tread carefully, cautiously and build my confidence. It's great, I help myself and others too. "Today I was talking to my good friend Karen. We have similar interests and understanding. We both are creative people, therefore seldom bored. She was telling me about the mysterious malady that affected her balance. "that's why she hadn't called." This has happened about the same time for the last three years. We had an unusual amount of rain this year. It was hot and the humidity was high, giving the air a tropical feel. Which I love, but don't get enough of. At any rate, working in her garden, she attracted all the mosquito and those little flying nits (no see ums) that swirl around your head, attracted to the scent of hard work.

She was determined to finish this garden, but she couldn't take it anymore. No amount of swatting off those little buggers for as tiny as they were—their numbers were great and they were mighty. There was no escape and no relief. She finally threw in the towel—I should say trowel. And, ran out of the gardens and scurried up the steps to the safely of her kitchen. Hoping those little buggers weren't following her. She breathed a momentarily sigh of relief But, the damage was done. She was starting to itch, her neck, her ears of all things. They are delicate. As the evening progresses, she started to swell. Well, parts of her face and her delicate ears. This went on for several weeks. Karen is brave, strong, relatively fearless (sort of like myself, so I understand). All those bites became toxic. When she would look up or turned her head a certain way would make her dizzy. The feeling of nausea was almost too much to bear. She lost 3 lbs. in those few days. "So Patti, that is why it took me so long to return your call."

That brought back memories of working in my gardens at my little cottage house. Me and nature. Nature always won out at my house. At least now, Karen was getting better. Not worse. "but you know Patti, as bad as I felt, there was no resting. I still had to carry on with things that needed to be done. I even finished the curtains in my reading room That wasn't easy for I had to constantly look up to see if the curtains were hanging straight. That made me dizzy and nauseous. But, I did it and lost 3lbs in in the process. And it does look pretty." "The funny thing is, she tells me--To me this strange malady, was almost like a vacation from all my other duties and obligations. I didn't have to go anywhere. I didn't have to talk to anyone. This offered me a good excuse." I laughed when she told me that. I understood exactly what she was saying. "you know Karen. We both are lucky. At least we have other interests that we can do in those times. So that offers us a distraction from the illness and helps us heal in the process Some people still have to go to work even though they are sick. And, when they get home, they have their family, the house, the mail etc. that always needs attending. And, if they can't it all just piles up. This was today, the 11th of July 2019. But I will continue with my thoughts of...

The last day of February 29, 2016 I had written. If this was a perfect world or we all had the good fortune or had the means or had the financial support from our own endeavors, spouse or inheritance we could all focus on our gifts. Maybe, we could be a little more generous with our time, money or put our energy to better use. Can you put a price on your gifts and talents naturally given? For that is a far greater gift than the monetary. Our creative endeavors will survive and continue in their element or fruition when healthy in mind, body and spirit. It's with gratitude when we use our gifts for the good. To bring inspiration, beauty and appreciation and finding solutions when working together in unity. It all comes down to a common denominator. And it can't be one sided, but shared.

55

Front Entrance and Mailbox

I was in the wonderful little town of Wayzata when I found a little shop that had mailboxes on display. One happened to have tennis players painted on the mailbox. I had one made. Seemed like a simple project but took weeks before set in place. Just below and to the right there is my sleeping cherub near the right of the steps. Sleeping under the mirrored window made from an antique window of a small church. From long ago.

chapter 7
DREAMS AND REALITY

I will continue to use my journal for this part is the first day of March 2016. Just a few tidbits for background, human interest and clarity. Getting through the long Minnesota winters that is not quite over but coming closer to the end as an enduring ordeal. Just getting through, a little wear and tear, feeling the effects of…but still standing and conquered once more. I've always believed in listening to your body. Is it overly or unusually tired? Are there little aches and pains that is constant, but bearable? Do these little messages affect my rest or my sleep? At this time, I had felt such an acute sense of weariness that I made an appointment to see my acupuncturist, Dr. Hu. I learned her practice was just moved to a different location a few blocks down. But, to me trying to navigate to this new location was a bit over whelming.

I actually I got there a few minutes early. Dr Hu was happy to see me. She has helped me through some of my most difficult times. She knew my background and understood where I was at in this life—my reason and purpose. That would continue to take its toll on me. She understood and assured me that I would persevere and get through. With her help, belief in me and encouragement I could carry on—do and be. She checked for certain vital signs. "Patti, you need to take some time to rest." She gave me a treatment. I lay there with fine needles—placed where needed, drifting in and out of memories and thoughts fleetingly. She quietly tapped on the door. It had been an hour, but it seemed as if a few minutes. She did tell me, "Patti you don't age." I told her it was my healthy life. I asked her if she wanted to see the lion I had painted. "Oh yes." She was busy. She could have said no. In my mind, I thought that seeing this painting would inspire her throughout the day. I had put pictures on my phone. I opened my phone and she caught her breath. "Oh Patti, he's beautiful. That is why you don't age." Keep doing what you are doing. I needed to hear that. Those words were so validating. To be able to paint that picture or write your thoughts, send that letter or just express, be creative in some form is not only worthwhile, but fulfilling and healing too. Mind. Body and Soul.

I felt so fortunate to have people in my life who care enough to share and are aware. Just taking that little extra time—can help more than we know. Before, I went home. I did a few errands and was to prepare for my trip to Tucson. I was to go to the caucus that evening. But everything took longer than expected. I didn't want to disarm my acupuncture treatment. That evening, I was to go to the caucus-- I realized that would be too much. I could not give or do more. My day was complete. I learned a lot that day.

I believe when we recognize the gifts we have been given and use them wisely and for the good, that brings inspiration and fulfillment into the lives of others. We also feel better about ourselves. Whatever our accomplishments will reflect who we are, sometimes even our intent. Maybe not immediately but down the road when the time is right. When we take time needed to write, paint or finish that project will give us a sense of serenity even contentment—for we are in the moment.

Why doesn't everyone know this? Why do we depend so much on man, our leaders, our educators—all the people we turn to for answers, solutions and even understanding of what we are doing? How can we when there are hidden agendas? That are not in our best interest. The focus now seems to prevent, hold back, control the situation, the outcome and the income too. Right or wrong, regardless. I remember when prayer was no longer allowed in schools or public places. Even the holidays or holydays were devoid of religious meaning. What an insult to our creator. But, our God, our Higher Power is waiting and watching for he is curious too. He gave us life—heart and soul, body and mind. We have a forgiving

God. But, what have we given in return? We need to be thankful, take care of and awaken from the slumber of apathy. 4/2/2016

The month of March turned to be disconcerting, so much so, I would only be able to write five more days in this month. And, then not a word until the month of August. I don't know if it was in the stars, the universe at odds or simply not meant to be. Whatever transpired in those months before and after seemed to set me up to fail and falter—never understanding the purpose or rational. But I had written the third and fourth day of March 2016. I had gone to Thrivent to talk over some business matters. That is not my realm of expertise. Financial matters have always left me drained. Hesitant to give my trust to those who lust-- after money. But appearances are questionable when delving further into the heart of the matter. I write, trying to get my financial life less complicated. In these times, when transparency went out the window. Never to return, but in a different guise, form or format. Whatever works. Appearance only. Who can we really trust? When those who had all the credentials necessary, also had their own agendas for profit only—themselves.

After those financial meetings that left me confounded. More confused than ever. I could say disheartened also, but I don't want to go there. I remember that one particular meeting, when I was losing trust. For it was always another complicated and monetary exchange. And, I was the benefactor. I'm listening but could I trust in this. I am handed these papers that I am to read and sign. After I read a few lines I start leafing through these papers. I felt a simmering rage. Maybe, this was not the right time. For me or for him. He had been gone, just returned from a big and important business meeting. Was this reaction from what I had heard through the grapevine? I looked at him, as he is seated in his chair, now looking more smoothed and polished then I ever noticed before. I stood up. Picked up my papers and start ripping these papers. One by one. As I'm lashing out my frustrations. My anguish directed to someone I had trusted and suddenly no longer. This was a complete shock and surprise for both of us. He is sitting there looking at me, speechless. As I'm ripping up these shards of paper, I'm so angry I could hardly see. "No, I will not do this. I won't be used any longer. This isn't going to help me. But will sure help your company." Now tearing tiny bits of paper as confetti. Tossing to the wind around the office floor.

I stopped my tirade. But, as I look at him, so composed with a hint of a smile on his face. Neither one of us knew what to say or do. I feel emotionally exhausted and embarrassed. As I look around. I see the shards of paper on the floor. I quietly say, now who is going to clean up this mess? He tells me, "my secretary will pick this up." That did not make me feel better. If he would have said, "I'll do it." I would have even helped him. Clean it up. But he is a man. A man with a lot of pride. I walked away. I stopped and looked through the heavy glass doors. He was on the floor, picking up the papers I had destroyed. I wanted to go back. Apologize. Help him. But, I couldn't. I felt my heart was breaking. What did either one of us learn that day?

60

For me, I learned and knew… I will always take a stand, once I recover my senses. I try and keep a certain distance, but important to know what is going on around me. Be prepared for the unexpected. See, that is why I don't like matters of business. So, I try and escape from that world. I check on my painting. He is beautiful, but like a lion, who is still a child. Should, I try to change him. Rearrange him. Or, keep him as is. To be as a symbol of life unspoiled. Not yet hardened. Still learning.

We will not always be naturally good or great at anything. But if we have the desire to learn or grow or even change our thinking it is possible. (If it is for the good and worthwhile.) It is about understanding the real reason and purpose in those endeavors. I also believe what we do in the arts, in our creative world is not limited in these areas…

For even the practicality or necessity of our business life, needs to have the same philosophy. If not will become ruthless. Letting in an element that becomes one sided and one dimensional. Where the rules change to fit the game. The game plan—winners and losers, all or nothing, sacrificing others even our sisters and brothers. But also sacrificing the best part of oneself. Creating uncertainty, walls of silence and avoidance, unspoken words meant to obscure for reasons unknown. Meant to be to protect their best interests and hidden agendas. No longer transparent or honorable.

Becomes confusing times when these practices become acceptable—for a price. Not detected because there are no consequences, only designer rules and regulations to insure the outcome. But when and how do we wake up the apathetic. Is it possible? Or do they even want to for their complacency is where they want to be. Don't rock the boat? Don't make waves. Until, adrift for too long, too far becoming unreachable and unteachable. We have to stop and think of how and why we have become so limited. Out of touch, feeling lost and disconnected. No longer capable. Until, we realize it is time to take that stand and remember our gifts are to be used for the good. And if not—stop and reevaluate thoughts, words, actions and deeds. For there will be accountability that will be met. If one cannot stop on their own—there needs to be an intervention and evaluation for understanding. We cannot repeat the same mistake when power becomes amuck.

61

Before my trip to Tucson there were house matters and business matters that needed my attention Leaving me with very little opportunity to journal. March 7th and 8th would be the last two pages I was to write for several months. For those precious blocks of time would never happen. During this time, before I was to leave, the weather moderated that allowed Billy to check on my house. For when I came home, and I looked up I could see Billy on the roof top.

This would be the last page of the March timetable. I wonder when we have too much going on in every area—not given enough time to even process. For one thing, not enough support. No one to turn to for guidance, encouragement or direction. Making these astronomical decisions left to flounder. Surrounded and fielded by predators of another kind. Waiting to make their mark. Professionalism finding another way. Contrary to when they started. Awakening another side more daring and not sharing. Times have changed when ethics and morals were thrown out the window. And this time, the field wide open for no one to stop them. Profit at all cost. And, at others loss. Not just for a few month or years, but this is the new normal. Where wrong is right. Get used to it. Get over it. Or should we? Think about it.

This was the time, when the heart and soul no longer existed in the business world. It was the bottom line--profit only. If not willing to play the game, by their rules only—in their broken state of mind everyone and anyone was dispensable. Controlling the outcome and using the wealth of others became the objective. It didn't matter the profit they gained. There was always a hunger for more. After much thought, I made my mind up to use another bank. For way too many reasons. Why did I stay so long? I wrote a note and added a poem that just poured out of me. For, I liked the people who I worked with at the bank, but it was the disregard and arrogance at the top. I could no longer tolerate. I enclosed this writing that once more became more like a poem.

"Boulevard Garden & a Touch of Wonder

There are many wonderful, beautiful and sometimes whimsical boulevard gardens though out the quaint little town of *Linder Hills*. I decided to add a little whimsey to the city for the little ones when taking walks with their family. Or for anyone that still is a kid a heart.

Painted Red Path leading to gardens

    I had painted the center row of red brick in the driveway. Sort of like the red carpet. I decided I would paint the pretend brick path with the leftover red paint. There was something about this little cottage house that heightened the creative buds. Becoming bold and daring with painting doors and floors. Anything that needed a coat of paint. I liked the results with this one. This little path led down to the gardens. To the right I had put steppingstones going to the window box. To the left led to the fairy garden, a bricked patio area and a koi pond. When having the time, working in the gardens was the most cathartic and relaxing change of pace. Very rewarding in the physicality sense to the depth of the soul for we are taking care of.

64

Ode to My Bank

I wrote a book of experiences—not to be known
I wrote another to enlighten my sisters and brothers
Along the way my experiences and story grew
The cause and effect—so many became
Eschewed
Not understanding left a void of uncertainty and
Ambiguity meant to shield, protect and perpetuate
Hidden agendas of those in high places
Who will continue to profit from denial
of their actions, becoming so entitled and
Prosperous and powerful too
When will we become brave enough, even more
curious to question and address—even step in
To clean up and clear up the mess
From dysfunction
Within these walls so high, Becoming
Unreachable, even unteachable
We all are affected in some way
By the cause and effect, left unchecked
And never address. We all play a part
In our children' future
We all can do and be better
Knowledge is the Key—Just knowing…

Patti Zona

chapter 8
IMPORTANCE OF AWARENESS

Now I am going into the 14th day of August 2017. The aftermath that would take my breath away. Leaving me to stop, at least a pause. Take a break from the constant onslaught that left me reeling. Not knowing who to turn to and having no understanding the purpose or rational of these experiences that affected every area of my existence. I always thought to do the right thing. If there was a problem address and fix it. Live within your means. Pay your bills on time, taxes too. Have consideration of others for we are all coming from a different place. We all make mistakes, but we try and rectify to find a solution that works for the best of all. The best outcome, being direct, transparent, fair and square. Having honor and integrity with respect and dignity intact. With no unexpected surprises, hidden agendas or lack of transparency in documents and transaction that will affect your life, your finances, quality of life, your health too. For, how much can we take before we break. And, it will and does happen in many forms. For stress comes to everyone in one form or another.

On this day, I had written in my journal. "I hope there are symptoms of recovery. It's a process. Discovery and recovery. The end of that summer of 2016, "after all was said and done" I started getting sick. I know it was the stress of it all. Coming from all directions, with no relief, no escape certainly no understanding. Or, I should say awareness from all concerned. I rarely need to go to doctors, but this wasn't going away. But the doctors that I did see were limited in their own knowledge. So specialized. I would be directed to a different doctor that might possibly know of this lingering ailment. I certainly wasn't getting better and of course— stress cares for nobody. It just magnifies the physical, emotional and financial aspect of life. I don't take medicines. But that of course was the natural recourse for most of these doctors. Try this pill. This should help. But whatever medicines or pill given would just produce further unusual side effects. Sinking me deeper into my strange ailment. After a while, I didn't think I was going to make it. My time was nearing. Was my time up? I would for sure have to get my affairs in order. I completely lost my appetite even for water, juice or tea. Just very little and that was too much. I was so tired, all I wanted to do was sleep. Rest was the cure. I needed to take care of me.

Even in my sickness, each day when I awoke, I would try and eat. Have a little something. But it was impossible. Food was foreign to me. Nothing tasted as it should, the texture made me feel sick. The slightest sugar, honey or slightest bit of salt was overpowering. Just the effort to eat or drink exhausted me. I would need to sleep. I would fall asleep in a deep slumber. When I would awaken, I would still have to sleep. I still had hopes and would try to regain my interests, brush my teeth, my hair. It was all so much work and so much to bear. I feel tired just writing about this. It brings back such memories. I never want to get that sickness again.

My senses or my delirium were heightened in some ways. The thing is I wasn't in pain. That was a plus, in fact, I was at peace and felt fortunate that I would be leaving this earth so quietly, gently and peacefully. I wasn't angry and I was never afraid. This just gave me an opportunity to prepare and savor. Each moment was a gift. I remember seeing a few dishes in the sink. I ran the water into the basin. The water feels so wonderful to my touch. As the water is coming down, I pour in a little dish soap. Tiny bubbles gracefully filled the air. I stop to watch and see the gentle beauty as a gift to me. I am mesmerized by the simplicity that touched me so. I even followed the one tiny bubble as he/she floated higher in the air. And then disappeared.

This went on for several month. In my mind this was a natural state of events. I wasn't getting better. I had this mysterious malady. The doctors were stymied as myself, yet I couldn't help but wonder, what part all that stress played in my life for so long. The cause and effect that was never addressed. At least I was at peace. But it wasn't over yet...

During this time, I also had a low-grade temperature that fluctuated. One night, I awoke in the middle of the night. I was soaking wet. My hair wet as if I had been in a shower. My jammies, my arms and legs. I jumped out of bed. "Thank you God. My temperature broke. I'm finally getting better." If that is all it took, I was thankful. For I thought I was on my way to recovery. But this went on for several weeks. It got to the point that I dreaded going to bed. Yet, I would be so tired, once I laid down-- I fell fast asleep. These strange episodes lessened with time. Eventually just disappeared as a bad dream.

But it wasn't over yet. Months later the pain came. Relentless. Day and night. Zapping pain, like electrical impulses creating spasms throughout my body. Usually my side was affected, but those zapping pains would strike anywhere and at any time. This went on for month—gradually subsided. But, sometimes would come back (not as strong) but as a test or a reminder maybe. I still carry certain effects with me. Weakness and motivation not the same. But, this weekend. I put on some of my favorite music. Making me want to dance. Without a care. Freely. Without pain. Is this a temporary thing? And, will I ever be the same? I doubt it. For we can't help but feel a little different, become more aware, a little more cautious, appreciate life more, more determined when conquering our fears, maybe be a little more passionate and might as well be diplomatic too. Whatever experiences we share there is an understanding. It's never too late to admit our mistakes for then we can move on and celebrate—life once more. This was written 9/3/2017.

The effects were evident in my handwriting as I'm going through my journal. The quote was interesting and apropos, "Creativity flourishes when we have a sense of safety and self-acceptance." But I must add it's not just our creativity—it's everything we do. But since I was still recovering and processing that strange illness. This is what I had written 9/3/2017. Lucky, when we have a safety net and can accept and be accepted. But what happened was life changing / life altering. How can one overcome months, a year and more of a mysterious malady that weakens and drains you? I am thankful for the moments of almost normalcy—giving me hope once more. I can and will recover. But it is up to me. I should know my own body, my own limitations. Be aware and take care. Or will doctors eventually work together to find the elixir that cures without the impossible side effects. The simplest thing for me—having a meal is such an effort. For there is no desire for food. Occasionally, I can eat a few bites of this and a few bites of that. It is as if a test. For how can I get my strength back if I don't get enough nutrients? I know this is a temporary problem amidst challenging times. And, it's really all these challenges meant to distract and take away from the important necessities in this life.

I noticed this book lying on my friends' table. It intrigued me. I picked it up. I mused to my friend. Have you read this book? "No, not yet-- it's my mothers' book. My parents were traveling to Europe visiting the Scandinavian countries primarily to know more of the history and culture." I leafed through the pages. "Do you think I could borrow this book? I will return it." Of course, he couldn't say no. This was a good thing. Something positive for a change. Norway set the example and the surrounding Scandinavian countries followed suite. I quietly read a few lines. "Their people are more productive, stress is not a factor, healthy, mind, body and spirit. Seemed to be the emphasis." Maybe I'm Scandinavian. I say with a smile. We need to speak up and out, if we are to have a future for our children. Meaning all children.

As I'm reading this book—it gave me some insight and hope. I don't feel so alone in my thinking. The thing is, we can learn from each other. It's not a perfect world. That is for sure. But If we put our heads together, hearts too for we care, our minds are capable. We have been given brilliant gifts that we are to share. And take care of to nurture and grow—healthy, in mind, body and spirit. We can do it. We can learn when given the right tools, practices and experiences that inspire. United in the same purpose and goal without hidden agendas meant to destroy—something. It's so much easier and gratifying to live constructively and productively. We need to know that what we do is meaningful and fulfilling. Giving our real reason and purpose a chance to take notice the importance and real value.

My life has changed so drastically. Yet, those changes as difficult as it was awakened something in me—like a bolt of lightning and thunder. So powerful. Yet serves a purpose and is a cause and effect from what is happening in nature. Nature plays a part as well as we humans. Reactions from events around us and that surrounds us. Sometimes without thought and no escape. So, we need to find a better way—to make these events and experiences work for us. For understanding. For what are the reasons we do the things we do? Can we learn from our mistakes? Can we address and correct without subjugation and shame? No one is perfect. But we all can learn to do and be better than this.

71

During this time of changes so profound (and not just overnight) for every day is a reminder of all the losses and those who gained. Did they not know there are responsibilities when reaching for and having successes that go beyond? Did they not know? Did they not remember there is a code of honor? A moral code which is rarely used. I made my decision to contact those who should know. Wake up and be more involved, more responsible. At least concerned. But in the hierarchy of life many are removed physically-- out of reach, out of touch. Then those who are just plain absent. Just not there without a care for they feel no responsibility. The designer rules were made especially for them. So, they have forgotten. But I would make one last attempt in this land of disconnect to address to those who have not been informed. Yet should be known of past histories for no regrets when problems are fully addressed. Then those mistakes are not continually repeated. Becoming a pattern of acceptance. That is why, I wrote my letter to Warren Buffet about my experiences with Edina Realty, jane Paulus and Ron Peltier. He would want to know about this. As I have heard, "he is such a good man." I believe so. But, is he aware? We all have responsibilities that just doesn't end there.

Of course, after sending that letter to Warren Buffet, I felt a responsibility to Ron Peltier of Edina Realty to give him the opportunity to address these things himself. I have given him plenty of opportunities myself. He was a busy man. But when he returned from his trip or this or that meeting—We would meet when he returned. That never did materialize. This went on for way too many months. Turning into years. I would get calls from his attorneys wanting to know what he could do. What did I expect Edina Realty to do? I wanted them to do the right thing. I wanted them to address this matter. To learn from this so no one else would be subjected to this disregard becoming a costly dysfunction. I had written about this before.

The designer rules were originally a temporary solution. Once, solvent their debts paid off and they were on solid ground— they would return that money to the people who were adversely affected. Instead of paying back, they kept the money and became wealthier than ever. No worries. For now, they were making millions. Becoming multimillionaires and billionaires. They joined the club of no returns. Yuk. Were they deserving or was the self-interest in their entitlements now the new normal? Wake up America. This has been going on for too many years. All the money in the world will never be enough for those who use and abuse the trust of so many. For they don't feel the pain of loss or regret for they are incapable. Their rewards have been too great and has any one really noticed? We have become so stoic. So complacent. Or is it unaware?

chapter 9
To Some One

I missed most of September, all of October and jumped to the end of November. In fact, this writing was on the 27th of 2017. It must have been of significance for it was of a dream that I still remember. I remember the colors. I was in a large room. It could have been a library with walls of shelves mixed with artifacts, papers and books. It was a hodgepodge. A little disarrayed, somewhat disorganized but filled with activity. It turned out to be a classroom—do your own thing. I lost my spot, my place, my space. I'm walking around, somewhat bewildered. I knew I was to be here, but I didn't know why. I'm confused as I start to leave. When, this helpful man stops me, "Patti, I found two paintings you have done. They are incomplete. But you have more than an hour to work on these. I was surprised ecstatic.

At this point in my dream, 'I'm standing on the ledge of a lofted area near a small ladder. This man seemed to know me, "let me help you down." I went to step on the little ladder and lost my footing. But I didn't just fall, I was rolling down, like from a hill. I roll down right into his arms. He's laughing and I'm laughing too. As if it was a most natural occurrence. And, I made it. I was so happy to be painting once more. The people around me were smiling, approvingly. I looked around for my brushes. My paints. Someone handed the two unfinished paintings to me. I look at them. Study them. They were familiar. A profile of a woman and a small boat on water--a placid lake. Interesting, I mused.

I didn't want to forget that dream. The feeling, the light heartedness, the reason or mission to create again.

I had just gotten back from Texas. My brother Rammy had just lost his wife of 51 years. It was such a loss. As always when unexpected. But I did see my family, from all over. Sisters and brothers and significant others, my nieces and nephews too. They remembered me or of me. Such a loving and vibrant family. I need them in my life. My artistic life. My creative life. How do I get them back, when scattered all over—everywhere. And, I've been here for so long. Maybe too long.

From my unusual dream to Texas with family. Now, it is Friday, January of 2018. I'm at my little cottage house. I had to write about this for it too, was something I knew I probably would never see or experience again. I wrote; Snowball in the Sky makes me happy.

I woke up this morning. Opened the shades from my bedroom window. I looked outside and saw a most wonderous sight. It looked like a giant snowball in the sky. It was a little after 8:00 in the morning. Could it have been a white moon—set against the light blue sky. My window faces west. I took a picture with my phone. Hmm, I'm thinking. Not sure. I went down the stairs. Opened my shades. It's been so cold, like below zero for too many days. These windows faced east. There was a bright shiny sun. Good day, I'm thinking. Now 8:35. I check the windows facing west. The snowball in the sky is still there. "It has to be the moon," I'm thinking. Is this possible for the sun and the moon to be out at the same time—so brilliant? I will find out. The sun rises in the east and sets in the west. Must be the moon, languishing on this cold beautiful morning. As a gift. A happy gift to all who sees or notices the snowball in the sky.

January 6th 2018 the next morning, I looked outside my window when I awoke. Not the same. I did not see the snowball in the sky. I was somewhat disappointed. But in my heart of hearts, I knew. I was just was hoping. That's okay, I'm thinking. I'm sure on another very cold morning it will reappear. Same time. Same place. Well at least it is going to warm up today—somewhat. Out east, there was super snow. Blizzard conditions. Here we have very little, just the cold. But I'm not complaining. Too much.

The month of January is almost over for it is now the 26th of January. I am thinking of sweet, precious Zoe. She just had a birthday. She turned nine. She had told me, "she needed a new apron." Momé You can get me a new apron for my birthday." I can do that. I happily tell her. She has such enthusiasm and awareness. She amazes me. Right now, she's a quiet wonder and delight. She continues to tell me that when she grew up, she was going to have her own donut café. I am so excited I tell her. For I love donuts myself. How precious these times are and yet so fleeting they need to be treasured.

I'm still in the process of recovering from my long siege of illness. I often wonder why I got so sick that I might not survive. But, I did. I'm starting to get my strength back along with a somewhat better appetite. When you're sick for a long time, it does take longer to be and feel back to normal. Sometimes, even better. But it takes patience and awareness of limitations. This winter we had very little snow, but also with extreme cold. Which presents other problems. But, this past Monday the 22nd we had a terrific snowstorm. With blustering winds. The snow flying sideway, swirling around. But, by 3:00 that afternoon it all stopped. Danny came and plowed out my driveway. He also took care of my lawn in the summer and the leaves in the fall. He was always dependable, reliable and affordable. He was also considerate about the noise level from the equipment he used—not to disturb or be invasive. How lucky I was to have such good people in my life.

Because, I was now plowed out, I could now make my dentist appointment. Just a checkup and a check. I have been to this practice ever since I moved to Minnesota. They take such good care and practice preventative also. Dr. Johnson was happy to see me as so many had to cancel because of the snowstorm. But, not me. I had my check up, teeth cleaned. And, everything was A okay. That is another area in my life that is caring, thorough, advocates preventative.

chapter 10

PLANNED OBSOLESCENCE

If only the financial industry and governmental would be more conscientious and especially responsible. But they abide by their own rules, privileges and agendas. As if so entitled. They no longer feel, worry or know of the struggles and losses of others. They tend to ignore problems, letting them grow. On top of that, they will even create problems for their own ego or distraction. Or is it for their own twisted pleasure and satisfaction. The thing is, we are all affected. Those who are experiencing, and those who see their fear and feel their despair and desperation. They want to help but are limited and don't have the means to intervene. Even if we do the right thing, can we trust those who can but don't or won't to?

Because of this new mind set of preservation with no checks or balances there are no boundaries or barriers for those who care more about the revenue or the bottom line. Without thought of their clients or the people who trust their expertise. They can only relate to the numbers, money coming in and wary of the money going out. Lust for more money to buy their power is their impetus. It's no longer about providing a means to achieve. But preventing real opportunities to come to fruition or even make possible to have a margin of success. Always at status quo. When we need to provide real opportunities for everyone. For there are no lenders, no providers or helping hand. Where can we find the help that is needed when it just isn't there. Not even in their thoughts. Relying on their wits to create as much havoc as possible to distract from the issues at hand. We need trust, competence and higher standards. Not scoundrels in the boardroom.

This is so hard. Not easy at all. How do I tell of my experiences that has had such a profound effect on not only myself, but many others? There is a responsibility in this life. No one is exempt. Yet, there are many who profit arising out of problems they created. They have the status, position, the means, connections and know how to manipulate to their advantage. They talk a good talk. They walk the walk and don't care if it's the walk of shame. They have nothing to prove for look at all they've done. All they have accomplished. Money talks, a walking talking living proof. If you play the game long enough, you will have the right connection and impression. Eventually, for people like to be impressed. It doesn't matter how you made it or degrade it. For some, that moment of glory is worth it all. Just don't have a face to the name or know anything about them. Stay detached whatever you do—keep your distance. Remove yourself. Don't answer the phone. Let your secretary screen your calls. You can't be reached. If you don't know—you don't have to feel or acknowledge in any way. Like a robot or robotic way of living. Might as well. There are no feelings there.

We've all been affected in some way from the dysfunction within the walls so high. Sometimes inadvertently, maybe ever personally. We keep our nose to the grindstone as a pretense to our busy-ness. Our productivity. We don't have time to feel, see or talk about the erosion of our conscience. We can't be bothered to try an understand—how we got to here. What changed us. Rearranged us. We used to feel but can't anymore. We don't want to be hurt. We don't want to be disappointed once more. I've tried but it doesn't work. But I have fame and fortune to my game. I just don't want to talk about it. These are just some of the scenarios to avoid—facing the music.

Okay this needs to be done. Needs to be spoken, talked about for clarity and understanding. There can't be a stone unturned. When these experiences are so far reaching, expanding even now. But, with a little more hesitancy. I've gone this far. I can't stop now. We just can't unleash and spill out the debris, rubble or garbage.

Then leave the mess behind, for someone else to step in undo the damage and unravel the pieces to pick them up and put them in their proper places. We need to look at our own part or role.

Were we aware of the red flags? Or did we ignore? Just not aware. Didn't want to know for then we would have to care. We all play a part in our ignorance and complacency. That is when we need to stop and recognize our part. Then to clean it up. Then clean up our selves. Inside and out. We need to stop living in pretense. I don't know what is so frightening about hearing the truths. Even more, knowing the truths so we know what we are getting ourselves into. To be forewarned to avoid the manmade obstacles in this life.

Haven't we learned by now avoiding our problems, not addressing them only lead to a bigger more complicated life. So complicated that we want to run away and leave the travesty behind. But we can't. We can't leave behind for someone else to bare the burden for then we would never learn these lessons. Our responsibility doesn't end and doesn't go away. Instead we need to address these mistakes and put them in their place. Then we can understand how and why we got here in the first place. If we had only known instead of being impressed by all the rhetoric. 79

I was using my journal throughout a good part of this writing, but I had to stop, for the memories and consequences are always evident. But we are in this life together. What we do. How we interact with each other—respect and consideration. It all comes to play. We are only human with human frailties. We will make human errors and mistakes. We will all need guidance at some point in our life. For every one of us. There are no exceptions. That is when we need good people around us to remind us.

But it is interesting in this time of disconnect. When a problem arises, it's not nipped in the bud. But it's allowed to grow and get out of control. We never questioned the dysfunction that continues to grow around us. Thinking it was beyond our control. We put our trust in man once more, for big money impresses. Do we ever stop to think where we are putting our trust? There is a Higher Power who is Greater than. He knows our heart. Why do we always ask for more, when there is no understanding and no gratitude. This was written the 24th of 2019 when the Mauler investigation aired. Isn't it ironic?

I will continue using parts of my journal as I have only seven or eight pages. This part was written January 26, 2018. It was a few sentences but so apropos. It seems, as if I have been surrounded by even more dysfunction. More pronounced the end of 2017. Now re surfacing as if needing to be addressed. The good. The bad. The ugly too. It's all playing a part in our lives—rearing its ugly head again. I didn't write again until May 8th 2018…

We had the longest winter, but spring is here, grateful to have survived it all. Even coming to an understanding and forgiveness. Because of my long illness I am going to try and sell my house. As wonderful as it is, it is a lot of work. Without any help but for a price. But people are in need of work that also provides a living wage. They are over worked and stress laden themselves. And it shows. Their gratitude, determination and thankfulness are always there. But the capabilities, time and support (help) is not always there for them either. We depend on each other.

At times I feel I am spread too thin, doing it all, being everything for everyone. We all need encouragement and recognition of some kind. Good work. Good job. So important. But, the busy-ness of our lives, the need for respect—civility is lost in the exhaustive state of being and always doing, on overload. Determination is always there. Patiently waiting for that break. Sometimes an awakening from the exhaustive state of mind, of being. Wanting to regain what was lost or taken.

I was thinking of trying to meet with Ron Peltier, about my house. I want them to do the right thing. The people involved in the sale of my house do have the ability and the means to do what is right for me as well. I want them to buy my house back. They could resale my house. Honestly and fairly. I paid too much for this house (I wouldn't have to go through the process of selling my house) This way, I could find another house more suitable. That was in my thoughts. My wish.

I can't believe that I was still writing about this, when I never had a response from the beginning. Why would the mentality change now? When they've already profited. The bottom line is their most important reason or incentive. Not doing what is right. Meanwhile, this becomes accepted practice while they continue profiting on problems instead of addressing them. I can't help but be angry about this. Profiting from dysfunction. When will we learn? Maybe, it is a mistake using my journal as a timeline of events. Yet it also provides documentation of when, who, how and why. It does bring an understanding and answers some questions. But I feel as if I'm in another quandary—how far do I go to reach, teach to provide the information needed for understanding? It seems as if an impossible task and so imposing. My pages from my journal are open. As if, beaconing me to continue this journey of discovery. For I am still learning myself. I had written it is May 26th 2018… 81

The last few weeks of May was unusually cold the winter lasting way too long. Now, the last few days of May has been in the nineties. My yard is like a jungle of giant ferns, hostas, peonies, lilies and vines of many kind. The trees now needing trimmed again. The work is constant at this house. Expensive too. To top it off, I had a mouse in the house. But not just a mouse, an infestation. They were here before I moved here. I had to have the ceilings in the lower level removed, cleaned up and replaced. Never in my wildest dreams would I believe I would encounter something worse than opening the pandora box of non-disclosure. Who in the world would know how to tackle this job? I would have an exterminator come every spring and fall. That was not his department. But he was sympathetic. "You'll need someone to remove the ceilings downstairs. Only on the lower level." The stress level was rising, I could feel it. The timing of these things never is fortuitous. How could I sell my house with a mouse or guess it would be a family of mice? This practically put me over the brink. I would have to hire someone. So, there goes another unexpected expense—that wasn't tax deductible either. Woe is me! I called Paul. He can fix anything. And, he doesn't complain.

When I told him what happened, he said he would come over after dinner to look at the scene. Some men are amazing. And he is one of them. If there is a problem, he will find it and fix it. And he did. It is done. He did the impossible. I could write more about this experience, but I need to get on with my reason for this book.

Soon after, I had a call from my artist friend Susan. I could tell by the tone of desperation in her voice there was something seriously wrong. "Patti, would it be okay if Tahlia and I came over?" From her work, she had picked up her daughter from school." I held my breath. What now? This had to have been important as I hadn't heard from Susan for a while. But life is busy for everyone. I've known Susan from the time that I had moved into Lake Point. That was over ten years ago. Tahlia was born with down syndrome, but her senses are keen. She loves music and painting. "like her mom." But when she walked into my house, I could sense a difference in her demeanor. Not the same sparkle or enthusiasm. Her sweet smile was fleeting. And she held back as if uncomfortable with her head down. Patti can we talk but not in front of Tahlia." I tell her. "I can set up an art area on the porch. She can draw and use the markers." But I could see the spark of creativity was not-- there was something more disturbing as Tahlia stands there quietly, submissively.

Something was terribly wrong. We set Tahlia up to do her drawings in the porch with nature close by. She was reluctant for she wanted to be close and protected. And we were, but what Susan needed to tell me—needed complete understanding of this delicate and sensitive revelation. I would learn that Tahlia had been abused. I didn't want to believe this. Years of knowing Susan when she was first pregnant to learning of her special child and her determination to make sure that Tahlia would grow up as normally as possible.

And she did, but now what has happened will it pull her in another direction. From losing trust of those who are to love and protect.

As Susan and I are quietly talking. I could see Tahlia looking up from her drawings occasionally. She could sense the seriousness. She gathered up her papers, with pencil in hand. Wanting to sit at our table to be with us. Now we could only talk discreetly and intermittently. Memories of Susan and Tahlia visiting my little cottage to see the gardens, sometimes doing painting outside and listening to music from Adele was Tahlia's favorite. Her little face would light up as she listened to her favorites. She loved that CD. Especially the piece (Rolling in The Deep and Rumour Has it and more.) remembering when her face would light up, with the biggest smile eagerly wanting to dance. She would take her mom's hand and mine and we would dance to the rhythmic sounds. The emotions the music brought to surface. Was it the rhythm or the feelings evoked that moved Tahlia so deeply? I wondered. From the time early on, I could see she was touched by the wonders that surrounded her. Music, nature or being immersed in her drawings and paintings left to her own imagination her unique style. Now their lives will change dramatically through no fault of their own.

It was difficult for Susan to speak of this experience. Being a single parent, her architectural studies plus doing her commission work to help with expenses and trying to coordinate it all for everything to come together. Never ending. It was amazing how she could do it all. But, the love of her child overcame and made it possible. And, was her inspiration, impetus her reason and purpose. She would not realize that those who should love and protect basically could not and were not capable. Did not have good judgment. Tahlia's father, to me did not seem to have a real direction in life. He worked as a bartender. Even though he denied he had a problem with alcohol. His actions proved otherwise. He was Tahlia's father. He deserved to have time with his child. But, no one knew about the other side of his life that was growing unnoticed and out of control. If he was to do work at bartending or something else—He would have his girl-friend watch Tahlia. That is when incomprehensible experience began for Tahlia and horrendous discovery for Susan.

At this time, they were living a nightmare. There would be testing and evaluations to be done. Even court hearings. Now living a life within a system that is supposed to protect. Eventually the judge made a ruling that the father was not to have Tahlia in his care. That was a sense of relief for Susan. Now on to healing. Everything involved in this time, took away from Susan ability to really focus on her studies even her work that had deadlines. This is where my writing from my journal took me. That stopped me in my tracks. How in the world do I even touch on such a subject? When I was talking to someone involved with my writing and I read a few lines. I ask, "Is this too harsh? Should I write about this?" I was surprised when he said. "Patti, that is wrong." But yet when he said that, I almost felt a sense of relief. "So, you don't think I should write about this?" "No Patti, this needs to be written about. What has happened is so wrong. You need to write this.

I am almost finished using my journal. But it was as if I was not yet finished, for it fell on this page when Susan would reach out to me once more. I was just starting to feel comfortable in my new place. Even planted morning glories in pots around my balcony. Climbing up the railings with pretty blue flowers unfolding peeking through the leaves. Just in case the morning glories didn't work out I planted petty pink peonies, begonia's that were doing quite nicely and planted a wire vine in a painted red clay pot made into a fish. He's mixed in with the flowers and doing quite nicely too. Oh, I also put a nice sized fern on the mosaic tiled stand and on the opposite corned I placed a tropical plant with blossoms of red. So, I have a flurry of flowers on my balcony that can't help but make me feel better. My friends like it too. So, inviting. This gives me a reprieve from the disturbances of the unexpected.

Susan had called but the very next day I would get a call from Billy. What would be needed from me now? For, I no longer had a house. I was now in my condo. As much as I missed my little cottage house, each day brought me to the realization of how much work amidst the seriousness of my life was a constant drain and strain. It was a call from a friend of his telling me that Billy was in jail. There is no pleasant or pleasing way to hear this or read about this. I can't believe this is my life. Extricating people from impossible situations to even providing financial help to them. For who are they to turn to in these times of disconnect. I'm not a therapist. I'm not a bank or an ATM machine that can spill out money. I would learn Billy was in the Todd County Jail. Sounds like a western movie.

When he called, he only had 15 seconds to tell me his tale of woe. It would take three calls in his desperate attempts for understanding. He would need twelve hundred dollars to be bailed out. Could I? Would I? And, even should I? Or, even can I? I said this before. Our country doesn't fix problems. They create problems and then profit from the chaos. I have always believed in preventative. That has never changed. I believe in getting to the root of the problem before it grows to out of control. To me that doesn't sound so impossible. But dysfunctions run deep and no one is exempt in this time of disconnect and discontent.

This is written from the last page before I sold my house. I had to go to the local hardware store, for in the stress of learning about Susan and Tahlia I had forgotten to turn the garden hose off and it burst. Spraying out water in every direction, but fortunately in a needed area. When I brought my hose, hopefully to be fixed. They insisted on giving me a new one. They were understanding. I decided since I was there and now had a few dollars to spare, I saw this dandelion stick—a picker upper of dandelions. So, you don't have to spray toxins in the grass or yard. Saves on the environment and good exercise too. I had one before but gave mine to my son in law. He really liked it. Hmm. That brightened my day. Even though I will be selling my house. I can leave it for the new owners.

The weather was unusually hot during this time. But the rains came and broke the heat. This part was written on June 1rst of 2018 with added thoughts or memories. To be able to be creative on our own time. In our own way. We are fortunate. But it is all the distractions coming from all directions from every source imaginable, I find it difficult and tiring. But we are all so different. For me, right now I need more serenity and balance. I want and need to have my life, my house and gardens in order, inviting and appealing. Inspiring and energizing when needed. It's not only a gift to me but to others. But I realize there is just not enough time or energy. Once the day is done, we are done and exhausted. We live in a topsy- turvy world—when rules have been made and broken. Replaced with designer rules for the select few --- I know one day we will get it right. But only when the light brings to the attention the problems that have been kept in the dark and unspoken. But, needs to be unleashed. The trust be known in order to correct and move forward with dignity. Is that not an impossible request? To me, it seems so simple. I do not understand ignorance in these times. But I do. We have information overload. Many times given erroneous information or misleading information even inaccurate info… How can we keep up? With our computers, our technology that comes also with all its new wonders but also adds distractions and complications in this land of disconnect in these troubled times. Which man made problem do we address first. How and why do people choose apathy over compassion and understanding. Or the importance of responsibility and what about accountability. What is that word again?

When people accept acts of injustice or harmful actions, when they look away or ignore—the big pretense. I'm exhausted by it all. Why do I feel so deeply? Is this all so futile? I look back at my life. It was never easy, who can you trust when those who are to love and protect were not capable—any longer. When those in position of trust betray our trust—and will profit from it. For we've become a business to others, another pawn to be moved or removed. To be acquired or dismissed. It happens all the time. Especially in the hierarchy of this life? Isn't that where we all want to be? To be given a chance in this fallen world. In this falling economy. Maybe we can fix it. But we haven't asked. Why do we put our trust in man when there is a higher power who loves everyone? But we forget that. We all are only human. We will make mistakes. At least ask for guidance...

Respect and Percipience

There is a growing need to understand and to be understood.
Why, when, where and what we leave behind
Is it precious and respectable or business
as usual and profitable too
for someone other than you and yours
what are valid reasons that make it so
when do we question to feel assured
once more, that the trust is still there but,
instead doubt and uncertainly fills the air.
What we leave behind is more meaningful
than we thought at the time. Why do we do
important things in such haste. When do we
learn from past mistakes. Where do we go when
when we've replaced. What made this so difficult
and hard to bare. This journey of discovery-- still
working on recovery. Almost there, a little respite,
rest and prayer. There is a reason in our purpose.

chapter 11
QUESTIONABLE PRACTICES

All we can do is try and stay centered as we go through this journey of life. Which is really quite remarkable when we let go and let God. Our higher power to guide and lead us, gently and quietly teach us. We will know when we feel that sense of connection and peace. It's not always there for we have forgotten. We are only human needing. We have momentarily lapse, sometimes for too long when we feel the sting or the bruising that is when we have to stop and process, evaluate and sometimes even reevaluate. It's like an intriguing study or lesson learned where you think you can't do anymore, go any further. Then we stop and are thankful, we go through, relatively unscathed, a little shaken but our resolve is still there.

There was a reason we had to go through all those blunders and mishaps. Showing us where our weaknesses are. Our problematic areas that are kept hidden because they can be helpful too, or useful later. Maybe we have a forceful personality, but basically a good and caring person. But through the years being demanding served you well. You spoke up when everyone else was silent. Maybe they were astounded, even dumbfounded by the audacity of your abilities and actions. Maybe they even wanted to test your limits. Maybe you were even testing your own limits. How much could one get away with before noticing the metamorphosis or transformation has gone too far? No longer likable. Becoming unlikeable to even oneself. We try and make up the difference, we pretend when we should be authentic. We laugh boldly when we should feel the impact or question what makes it so… To make up for the loss we consume more goods, relics, latest and greatest gadgets, toys of all kinds, big and small, boats that float and yachts that impress and to express—

that's what it's all about. But, it's really about the bottom line that says and does it best. Just getting there—an adventure. The rewards great and the monetary even greater. A major triumph and to think never having to be responsible or ever to be held accountable. The sky is the limit. But not really. For there is an awakening—one day.

But what happened to all those people, who worked hard all their life to help make it all possible? Even made it happen. What happened to them? And why didn't they know better? That is a question or a mystery to some. But, shouldn't be. Especially in these times. There are artisans and craftsmen. Dreamers and schemers, scholars and lackeys, those who aspire. To those who inspire and those who perspire getting there, getting it done. Sometimes with blood, sweat and tears. Then there are users and abusers, why weren't they stopped? Why are the rewards so great for those who take? With the changing of the guards, added to all the new technology just opened the doors wider for those who equated money with power. So many changes that helped further their cause and create a wider gap and disconnect. Leaving the people in shock and disbelief with nowhere to turn. So, it appears to be.

We could have thrown in the towel or the trawl. Depending if they could clean up the mess or catch the vermin at their worst and have them pay their dues. Admit their follies. Clean up their act with restitution that is acceptable and plausible, fitting the crime. As I'm reading this, I wonder if I'm starting to get delirious instead of serious. I feel as if I'm a fisherman. Maybe even a cowboy I should say cowgirl writing this segment. I could be a little over wrought, over done or over tired and overspent in more ways than one.

Has anyone noticed the changes around them? People ask me what I feel when I read or hear about another senseless act. I tell them," I do feel angry. But more than anger I feel saddened." I also feel ashamed that we still haven't learned after all these years to take care of the responsibilities at home, our schools and our workplace. Instead we are removed not valued or recognized in our real purpose. To be forgotten. We cast aside what was and is needed most to build that strong foundation that provide and keep those healthy values intact for guidance. Instead we've turned our attention to preserving whatever quality of life we still have for the sake of our dignity and future for our children.

Just keeping the necessities in this life amidst the addictions that have become out of control, harmful and dangerous too. Yet those harmful elements are never removed. They've become profitable and serves those who provide another means to control. Being under the influence of anything or anybody only leads to dependency and brokenness. We are living in a constant state of fear and uncertainty. That is not a healthy way to live in any society. We continually look the other way for we don't want to know or be involved in anyway. Ignore and ignorance goes hand and hand. We give our time and money to create massive amount of highly addictive drugs to feed to the weak and weary. Doesn't matter what status.

Now on to the NRA. That our government seems to hold in such high esteem. Who are they afraid of? If anything, they should be afraid of themselves. They've become merciless mercenaries, without a heart, conscience or soul. I was told, because the NRA has so much money. They also have control of our government. That is nothing to be proud of. That means our country has stock in weaponry all the ammo stocks and barrels. The NRA has total control of arms that are sold and distributed to anyone. We have more guns in this country than any other country. Not just a little gun, but guns of massive destruction for one purpose only. And, anyone can have one, two, three or more and out the door. Yuk, I do not like writing about guns. They are ugly and destructive. They don't preserve life. They take life. Innocent people, children and babies too. Stop the madness. Get out of town. Get out of Dodge. Go to the moon. You can practice all you want but not on this planet. For crying out loud life is more important, valuable and sacred than the blood money that is in your pockets or your purse.

Ladies you're not exempt from this. We are the species that is supposed to have heart and common sense. Do you remember we are the nurturer of our children and for those who need comfort? We naturally provide the care needed but now it's a big trade off. Competing for a man's world. In a man's world. Sacrificing your femininity while ascending the corporate ladder. Do you look around you in your loftiness? Sure, you can do. But you have nothing to prove. Women can. We are capable. This is just a test of your willingness. Are you willing to step on others to get to the top? Are you willing for a price to sacrifice your most prized and precious? Because that is what is asked of you. I know you feel a responsibility to all the women in the world. Or maybe this is your own personal private goal. Ambition. Ambition comes in many forms. Whatever we do, we do it honorably, respectfully for the good of humanity. And always be thankful for your gifts.

Now for the male species. All you men. It hasn't been easy for you in these last ten, fifteen, twenty or thirty years. Opportunities were abundant especially in the eighties and nineties. And then the year 2000 successes so many, changed you. Went to your head. It was the me generation and you took it literally. I always think of that song "It's not about me. It's all about you. Why can't you see, what can we be so it can be we." Please." I change the words a bit. But, when any of my friends seem to be full of themselves, filled with pompous and pride. I will sing just a few lines, to remind them—life is about everyone. About we. For we need each other. Sometimes they laugh depending on the depth of the seriousness and determination.

You men really band together, support each other and have each other's back. That is a beautiful thing. Your loyalty to each other is more usual, more so than for women. But we are probably, it looks like it, they say it is so—that we are better communicators. Could be. I know there are insecurities for opportunities have been stripped away from you. Leaving you in a quandary, how to fill in the gap, replace what is no longer viable. Not only are we women taking over many of your jobs. It is an empowering trip for them. And somewhat agonizing for you men. I can sympathize I can see and understand your plight. Not only do women want your job or your role, but robots too. Computerized world we live in has caused a lot of problems and frustrations. So, eager to get the latest and greatest technological gadget (toy) out there, we outsourced the best of us and our favorites, tried and true for instance television, typewriters and CD players that could rotate six of the favorite cd's. I miss that.

All these changes happened so quickly. One day it was here on display. The next day disappeared in the dust of ruins. For no longer was there a technician who knew how. Planned obsolescence. You should have warned us. Then we could have planned and taken a course on how to repair. I know it wasn't completely your fault. It was the communication thing—not wanting to confront and see and feel the disappointment. So, you just let it slide into oblivion. And to be fair. Because of the uncertainty of the economics and rapidly rising dysfunction and corruption in the most unlikely places there was a lot of instability. All the tried and true were being replaced are now misplaced. Wondering what their purpose is to be now? A computerized world filled with new technology. New skills to be learned on the job training. But, specialized. Don't go any further. That's not your job. Which is stifling your mind, your body. How can one grow and learn when one dimensional? How can one be excited about their work when no longer inspired? Doing the same thing repeatedly--over and over again. Repetition and redundancy over time becomes overuse. With very little pay certainly doesn't keep up with the growing cost of inflation. Shouldn't this have been studied and investigated more thoroughly before leashing it to the public—everywhere. And not prepared. And not forewarned of the cause and there will be affects. The thing is these problems or red flags were never addressed but allowed to grow. People noticed, but not the depth of the problems. Never got to the root of the problem for understanding. Now businesses were formed from the chaos, the brokenness. Thrown together for appearance only. A temporary arrangement. But not a solution. Just testing the reaction and biding their time to once again get their affairs in order. They would be one jump ahead, one step further to no returns. Sometimes our memory

93

is short. We forgive. We forget. We get busy and we never lose hope for we are patient. Abiding our time. What have we all learned? Those hard lessons of no returns. Fortune waits for those who take as a test of willingness when for the love of money is greater than their heart or soul.

Their needs to be accountability in the mix of responsibility. Did they deserve it? Did they earn it? Did we forget we bailed out those who used our trust and funds? Did they forget that they were fortunate to be bailed out by their sister and brothers who were now struggling? They never noticed and never gave back in their entitlement and golden package of designer rules. Meant exclusively for them. They would not fail. But what did they lose in the process and what did they learn? Has anyone ever questioned how much was gained? How big was their profit? And, how and why did they become so entitled when they were the cause of the collapse? Is the dysfunction and corruption so widespread, so deep that it is impossible to repair. I doubt it. Just address and correct with restitution for those who have been victimized by a system that failed to address.

The thing is no one will ever be their best or give their best when living under a dark cloud of worry or shame. Sure, there will always be those who love those numbers the higher the better. That is what they strive for. Doesn't mean for their love of money they can take and never replace. They still are to share their knowledge and the importance of growth. Not just the acquiring of, but their real purpose. To be used for the good of mankind / humanity. Our children's future. It is an awesome responsibility to be a leader, teacher, mentor and homemaker. Yet, really not recognized in their importance and contribution to society. For the bottom line always seems to be the impetus. The main objective. But the erosion of society starts with a shaky foundation unattended. Struggles too many and for too long—without a break. When the moral code of honor and respect for life no longer exist. We will slip—if we don't take care of each other. We will fall. For, we all were given the gift of life. What we do with the gift is our gift to each other. Always with gratitude…

94

"

My favorite place, where we all gathered or gravitated to entertain or be entertained. Music for me is as necessary as breathing. To the left of the piano and on the window ledge there is a classic little car, with a push of a button would play "Slow Rider," the kids would dance to rhythm and laugh in the moment of it all. Looking out the windows to gardens, a small fairy land. Oh, there is one of my paintings on the wall. So, a very inspirational little house. Everything within reach."

chapter 12

DISRUPTIVE PROJECTS, IS IT NECESSARY?

I did get off the beaten path but will continue with August 14, 2018. I had written, I have a closing this Thursday the 16th. I will be selling my little cottage house. It must be, for I have been sick with something for over a year. I believe the ongoing stress from the time of moving in and will I be able to make it when I move out? The emphasis in selling a home now a days is on of course the appearance of the home inside and out. Has it been maintained, well cared for but also have curb appeal? Most people do take care of within their capabilities and affordability. But what disturbed me was their (the realtors) insistence in the buyer and seller were not to meet. Why was that? No one knows the home better than the owner. Sometimes I would not be able to be at my house. But there were those times there were so many showings that it was impossible to leave. I had to be there. As a matter of fact, that was the most satisfying aspect meeting and talking to the possible new owner. Some people meeting (me) the owner was the best part in their decision. You should be there.

I like positive experiences to know and grow. To envision and have an idea giving more meaning to embarking on such an endeavor as buying your home. You want it to be a positive experience for the buyer and the seller—not kept in the dark. Buying and selling a home should not become another business for the banks and wall street to profit once more. For everyone needs a home. Work together-- the buyer, seller and realtor with transparency. No unexpected expensive surprises. For, most people it's the biggest investment they will ever make. This was the oldest house I ever bought. It's interesting learning who owned my house before me. It's part of history. In the making...

My little house was a unique house. It stood out in its charm. Instantly a desire to create, add to and have your dream home. I was not alone in my choice or my vision. Linden Hills this community itself nestled amidst lakes with walking paths, shops and restaurants and coffee shops, local co-op and very own Sunnyside Gardens with a friendly and helpful hardware store that I could walk to. Everything that is needed or desired in walking distance. Now that is special. The ambiance in abundance and getting your exercise too. I lived one block over to the new and improved tennis courts. Now vibrant with eager new players to enjoy and advance to each level of play. One big city block offering tennis and many amenities for children of all ages. A ballpark for budding young player and an inviting little park for the children to play and a wading pool for the little ones to splash and cool off on those hot summer days. Parents, kids to meet and greet, building new friendships with warm memories to share.

98 I can't help but expound on all the virtues and the nuances of Linden Hills. From the times I moved to Minnesota years ago, I was intrigued by this inviting little community. The perfect place for anyone and everyone. A mix of homes, small and smaller the perfect starter home. Or just plain cozy, unpretentious. Yet still having its own unique quality. There are schools in walking distance with buses to bring when choosing this school. There are several different churches providing an instant feeling of spirituality. Taking a walk on a Sunday, I loved the little church on the corner of Beard Ave and 42nd street. Just one block from my street—Abbott. The people in the parish maintained the grounds lovingly. The music or voices singing giving praises would make me stop to listen and be thankful. Once more. But there were also grand stately homes that were in this little community. All together compliments and complimenting a unique and gracious was of living. I miss it so…

But time has a way of bringing changes. I don't mean the natural changes but man-made. And, not always for the better. For there is an agenda that has not been well thought out. Man gets in the way with his daring dreams and dubious schemes and his big money given to implement ideas. Big changes that will be profitable for himself and the big and small government. They hope. This is just an experiment you know. Let's see what happens—the reaction. Will there be?

Begin slowly, get to know the lay of the land, the people. Are they amicable? Are they pliable and could or would they serve their purpose? How is their health? Are they aging? Are they prosperous or having some financial struggles—now? No longer is it about just selling your home but changing the lay of the land. Adding a type of mix off beat modern feel built precariously closer than necessary— like making this big presence known. Like it or not. Someone will buy it for a price that makes a statement. Encroaching boldly invading the space available now fitting tightly almost against the original brick or stucco home next door. Even the stately grand home is diminished. Disregarding the past, the history and the original intent—affordable homes for the hardworking people in an inviting space. Is it possible to maintain? You could tell, this new look is forced without too much thought beyond the revenue. Now feeling a bit bewildered instead of inspired. It doesn't feel good. It doesn't feel right. What is happening? In this land of uncertainty? Are we becoming too fragmented and out of touch? Maybe. Discombobulated.

Hustle, bustle with lots of trusses tearing down to develop something big and boxy. Paint it stark white. Oversized windows, not a whole lot of character. Got to keep it big and sparse. Keep the construction cost low as possible, but with a hefty price. It's not the developers concern and obviously not the state governing concern either—that the inviting character is being lost in the big ugly. That is overpriced. But, good for the state because they can raise their rates. Once more the taxes can rise. Dysfunction just keeps growing. Not just in Minnesota. Even though for me that is where I learned firsthand about the dysfunction and corruption in America. At the time, I thought it was easy enough to address. Because, I thought we all knew better and nip this dysfunction in the bud, before it got out of control. But that didn't happen. They let it slide as if the biggest thrilling ride. They survived and craved that high. Let's do it again! For there's no boundaries here. The skies the limit. No one to stop us. For look we impress or is that surprise and wonder or shock and disgust. Can't be that for look at our rewards. Recognition doesn't matter that it does not flatter.

There could have been a better way, a more respectful way. Given a little more thought. Stop the madness before you go any further. You've made enough profit. You can afford to lose something. At least give back. Look at what you've taken from others without a thought. Now is the time to make restitution for your poor behavior, neglect and recklessness. Be an example of goodwill instead of letting your greed rear its ugly head. The results of your actions and expensive enterprises are too costly. Hasn't anybody told you that before? You just didn't know? You were not aware? Then it is not completely your fault. You should have been taught. Learned a more understanding and compassionate way. You just needed a reminder, some guidance. We all do at times. As if a child. Growing. Learning. Excited about life. But still needing direction. For we don't know everything. We are still learning ourselves. And this is just about the dysfunction in one area—that housing market the way things were and still are done. And it's done poorly without thought or consideration. It only reflects what you and we have learned or experienced from…

Corporate America, wall street, the banks operating with a single mindset that is acquiring more. Doesn't matter how. Doesn't matter if there is a need or because of entitlements. Aren't you lucky? You don't have to be accountable or responsible. And it shows in our falling and failing economy, the imposing debts bestowed to our young people to cover your own impossible missions of default. You're not affected. But you are. We all are. We have lived with the results of your careless and reckless decisions made. But you're showing your true colors and they aren't pretty. Not a good combination. You have to do better than this, if you want to go down in history as a great leader. Look at what you have proven and shown is all areas of this life—not only the housing market. That was only a steppingstone to your agenda or plan gone astray.

For the door was opened to the rampant greed affecting medical care, specialized to nonspecialized and unsterilized dangerous, too many, too much all about the money now and what can be gained. At the costs of people's lives and their minds too. That is unforgiving when the money made comes before the value of life itself. When, why and what changed the mentality of the pharmaceutical and insurance becoming not only addictive but harmful too. Along with cost prohibitive. But what can we do? It is no longer about the quality of life or saving lives but again the revenue. Now put in the bracket of questionable rackets (and I don't mean tennis, bad mitten or ping pong) but racketeers and marketeers. I have to be so explicit as not to be misconstrued or misunderstood. So, there is no denying the importance of what we do.

Now to get back to selling my little cottage house. I hadn't quite sold it yet. But thinking back leaves me still rather perplexed from the very beginning of buying this house. I paid more than I should have. Yet, I trusted wanting to believe this house would have no serious or expensive problems. Otherwise, why would it be priced so high. Originally it had been on the market for over 500,000 dollars. I was able to have the price lowered somewhat. But would learn I still paid too much. I bought this house in October of 2006. Prices were still higher than should be but was also starting to go down. It wasn't until the economy crashed in 2008 that everything fell. Especially effecting homes. I had just moved in.

Learned from the beginning my house was fraught with serious problems. I had bought a house for way too much money with non-disclosed problems. When I initially bought this house there was plenty of time for the owners and the realtors to say, "Wait a minute. Here are somethings you should know before buying or signing on the dotted line." I only had a month to move. Even more so I should have been warned of what was ahead of me. But that would never happen. A month is never enough time to move from a house for the seller or the buyer. But felt it was odd how things happened so quickly that the sellers weren't even at the closing of this very special house. (red flag) They quickly packed up their things and moved out. Moving out of state. Now, I was told unreachable.

There were several reasons why this would become a very expensive endeavor for me. I was going into the unknown and undisclosed arena of life. When from just learning the money that was to be used for the down payment of my condo was not there. Never put into my condo. I no longer had any money to put in any house. Was this part of the designer rules that would fuel the housing market to insure their profit from the unsuspecting buyer and seller? I wrote about this in my second book. In fact, I was finishing up my first book when I moved into my little cottage house. But would complete that book at my little cottage house. When I finished that book in a flurry of frustration—I realized I had to write another book about the experiences of buying my little cottage house.

I wrote both of those books to enlighten and empower people with valuable information they could apply and use throughout life. But also, to awaken the consciousness of those who were the root of these problems. Writing under duress and frustration was quite the undertaking but I was determined to get through this intact. Because these experiences that were so profound and costly became my impetus to write and expose these problems that would erode quality of life and our funds. When transactions are no longer transparent and ignored the problems grow leaving serious problems behind with consequences for years to come. Becoming widespread and far reaching. And if not investigated continues to be profitable for big business. Government too. All involved. Somewhere, somehow my books were held hostage instead of out there for my experiences to be known.

From the onset, from the beginning of buying my little cottage house. Once more I would be challenged with very little left to give. Just moving as a single person is difficult enough. Life is busy for everyone. Memories of moving to my little cottage house could not help but surface. Like it or not. They were there to remind me not only of my challenges, but the transformation and restoration that was done continually surprised and inspired me further. Even though my funds were limited I had good people helping me (they needed the work themselves) and I would pay in installments until completed. It did take longer, but always a little more progress. Plus, a natural diversity for they could continue with other jobs or work needing to be done. Also, giving me time to write my letters, work on my book and do all the necessary things that was needed attending or attention.

Therefore, knowing that I could make my little cottage into a most inspiring and inviting place was important to me. At this time, I need to say or add—I did try to get a loan to get all these things done. But, my bank would not. Complicated and convoluted, confusing too. For their marketing stated their generous loans for those who were approved. I always paid my bills. But I didn't use credit cards. The money gained from credit cards was more profitable for them. I wasn't going to play their game. They had taken enough of my money and more ways than monetary. Now what was their purpose? And didn't they even know or care?

A smaller bank was recommended to me. The person I was working with to get this accomplished was understanding and was for sure that I would get this small loan. 15,000 or 30,000 would really be helpful. That would be helpful to everyone. When Brad called me, I could hear the disappointment in his voice. I would not get the loan. I think I felt worse for him than I did for myself. Soon after, he stopped working for that bank. But he did call to tell me if I needed future help to call him. That was nice, but I decided whatever I did I would do it myself. I would find a way. For I did get every two years a very small cost of living but would never cover the rising cost of inflation, but I could do it. I will get by. I remember when banks were providing a service to their customers. They valued their clients. But that changed with big money, especially after the collapse of 2008. Finding new nefarious ways to make banking more profitable for themselves. While using the moneys from the people, through buying homes, to student loans, through every transaction big and small for millions use the banks. Every transaction made. They would be paid. They learned that when the government bailed out the banks and big financial institutions they would not fail.

I lived in my little cottage house for almost twelve years. I still would write my letters amidst the turmoil and the distractions of my life. I never let those challenges overshadow the positive changes made in this time. For each trial and error, I would learn something. Maybe something profound and so unexpecting I would have to explore the reason. The purpose between these actions and transactions too. So many of these actions and interactions from the brightest to the most humbled would affect my life so profoundly that it seemed my senses were heightened further.

104   What was I to do with all these new insights and revelations that have come into my life? The thing is, what I noticed the brightest star was sometimes too strong in its presence. Always wanting to impress, be heard and be noticed. Those who had to withstand the trials and challenges for one too many times-- waiting to be heard, wanting to learn how to do this life and regain their dignity for they had lost so much already. All they needed was someone in their corner. Someone they could trust. Someone who could see their strength, believe in them giving them hope. It's not easy in this world of disconnect. When those who can. Refuse. Don't want to know. Until it touches them.

Now getting back to the closing of my condo I had decided to buy. This was last year on a Thursday, August 16th 2018. I still was feeling the effects of my long illness. I kind of wanted to savor the time still here. Yet, enjoy the process. Which is hard to do when you're told what to do. If you stay you feel like an intruder in your own home. Don't speak unless spoken to. If you are to be home, try and stay invisible, as much as possible. Well maybe not quite that bad. For I did enjoy meeting and talking to the cute couple Belle and her husband Yan. They were looking for a home for their daughter and son-in-law in California. I liked their enthusiasm. I also had a second showing with a young couple. They were expecting their second child with their little girl in toe, carrying her little doll. When they left, they had forgotten her little doll. Left behind. Until I noticed this little doll, I call out to the parents as they are getting into their car. You forgot your sweet little baby doll. They came back carrying their child. Her little arms outstretched. She knew herself that she had forgotten but didn't know how to convey to herself or her parents. Now she was just happy and content. Everything and everyone in place.

I had three showings that day. Good things happen in threes. I do believe. This was when I met Jeanne and Art who were drawn to my house. We didn't talk that much, but I could see a sense of humor in Art's demeanor that lightened the mood even more, bringing a natural levity. His wife Jeanne had more of a quiet, thoughtful and reflective presence. I liked her. I liked her intellect. Her observations were keen with a respectful outspoken manner that was refreshing. There was such an interest in my house that I knew things would be happening soon. They were gracious and I was thankful that more people than not could see the creative wonders of this little house. And was drawn to as well as I. Tracy, my realtor would tell me-- she felt we would have a buyer very soon. That I should prepare myself, make it easier also to leave before actually being sold. Encouraging me to find a place that could replace, relocate. Shield myself from the experience of selling my little house that I had put so much into for almost twelve years. Seemed like a lifetime. Why did I feel so sad? Was my illness playing a bigger part of this decision? Is that a good enough reason? For I could get better if there were no stress.

I would have mixed feelings—needing to sell my little cottage house. Yet wanting to linger and stay to enjoy the fruits of my labor. Isn't it ironic, I am thinking to myself? Ever since I bought this little house, I would have someone a realtor usually and even a developer occasionally wanting to see my house. Initially when

105

this occurred, I just thought my little house was so unique that it naturally piqued their curiosity or interest. But it happened so frequently that I realized it was just their business. The numbers you know. I was curious myself when the developers would call and want to see, survey the scene. That is when I learned their interest was in buying and tearing down. I cringed at the thought and angry at their audacity. But upon seeing my house, they would tell me that my house was too nice to tear down. They would not do that. But if I needed to expand upstairs that was an idea. I appreciated the fact that they recognized the uniqueness of my little cottage house. But the fact that this was so rampant made me a bit wary. Especially the different realtors calling to see If I was ready to sell my house. Even when I had first moved in it did not matter. Even when they knew I was in the throughs of the restoration. Their eagerness over road their good judgment. But this was after the collapse of the economy and everyone was desperate. My curiosity was piqued myself, so I would listen to their spiel. Maybe this would solve my problem. Sell my house as is—but what I learned-- if I sold my house at that time, I would owe money to the bank. For the price of houses went down and would continue to depreciate. They were desperate for houses to sell. And buyers needed a house they could afford.

I would find a condo in Edina not too far from my little cottage house—ten minutes or so. There was lots of construction going on. But then again for some reason there would be excavating of streets, bridges, so lots of detours. Around the curve you would marvel and wonder of the cavernous holes and mounds of soil, sand and piles of dirt, depending on the location. Huge hunks of concrete that looked rather foreboding leaning this way and that. Seemed the whole state of Minnesota was under siege now a giant construction zone. How could one see or visualize the lay of the land or capture the magnificence or ambiance beyond the rubble before them? The noise from all the different machinery doing their thing. Creating more dust then was healthy. This was a temporary inconvenience, distraction. When it is all said and done, will be so worth it. You will be happy here. Once upon a time, this was like a dream. When I wake up—will be over.

Each day would bring a change. Interesting. Progress. But then another house torn down, another street filled with cones. Most standing upright, a few fallen on their side. Fleeting thoughts of stopping and picking them up and putting them in their proper place would come to me. Of course, I didn't do that. What good would that do anyway?

Amidst it all, I did find a condo that would work eventually. After the processing and everything you go through after any big change. When driving into this complex, to the right there is a Library, to the left there is a four storied red brick office building. In the center is a parkway with trees and shrubs of various kind accented with variety of flowers. In the middle of the parkway there is a sculpture of Humpty Dumpty sitting with his skinny legs crossed reading a book. Whatever he is reading gives him a sense of reverence and deep thought with his reading glasses slipped to the tip of his nose. When I walk through that little parkway, I stop and rub his bald pate for recognition of appreciation. I like the whimsical within the elegance. Setting back are three separate buildings four stories high. All three building are slightly angled. And all have different views. One of the building is encased with a dark green tarp. With scaffolding in surround for workers to remove the offensive stucco. The building where I bought had gone through the same treatment the year before. Once they are finished will never have to have this done again. Thank goodness.

The day before the closing we had a walk through. It was a nice sunny day with a gentle breeze. When I got to my soon to be condo, I could see the smiling faces of my realtor Therese and my daughter Monica and the girls Lucia and Zoe waiting in anticipation. Everyone is busy, time is of the essence. Yet, taking time to see and be part of made this a little more special. We first walked on the main level through the great room, a grand fireplace, comfortable seating and a room with walls of books. Like a library. We walked over to the large windows and glass doors looking out to an inviting patio with a large pool of water. A spray of water coming from the center of the pool with a family of ducks gracefully floating in the midst as if a special attraction. A comfortable place outside to take a break, read or visit with friends. We would not linger as we headed for the elevator to take us to the fourth floor. The hallways were spacious with columns after each unit lending an air of stateliness. And a large window at the end of the hall adding natural lighting. When looking down and through the trees we could see Our Lady of Grace Church. The church we went to as a family and where I taught C.C.D. (religious education) for nine years. We all liked that. Very gracious

We opened the door with lots oohs and ahs which is always nice to hear. We went to the balcony looked over the railing. Momé you've got a train track. I certainly did. Like going back in time. And, Momé look that shrub is shaped like a heart. Sure enough. I felt a quiet happiness. I think we all did at that moment. To the right was a grove of fir trees with nicely landscaped surroundings. We went inside to see the bedrooms and all the walk- in closets. Even my office had a walk-in closet, which I think I will convert into a small library for books and artifacts. Everyone was impressed with the size of my kitchen. I could have a party or gathering. I even had a laundry room that you could walk into and even hang a few things that you don't want to put in a dryer. Pretty nice. This was a very comfortable space. The large windows were facing north but slightly angled east and west. So, I would get early morning and late afternoon sun. Which I learned was perfect for more flowers than I thought. We departed with happy hearts just seeing and knowing all was going to be well. A good life. That is what I want for all.

Knowing the next day would be my actual closing, I went directly to my little cottage to start preparing. I wanted to do this in the best way and least stressful way possible. Once I was home did a few things bringing thoughts and memories to mind. Processing the past and the here and now. I even found my little angel key ring

I had been saving ever since I moved here. Now to be used for the new door. Simple things, simple acts can give me such a quiet joy. Like a message of good will, peace and harmony knowing there is a reason and purpose. I had written, always to be surrounded by angels. I do believe God sends his angels to help protect and guide us. I know God is my protector. Otherwise, I would not be here. I have to remind myself to take care for I am only human. And feeling tired. The top of my head hurts. A sharp little pain. I call it a zipper headache. Fortunately, it doesn't last long. Just zaps me with this sharp feeling and travels down to the base of my head. And, is gone. Depending on the stress level there could be several bouts or none at all. This was on the 19th day of August 2018. I had written, "yesterday all my troubles seemed to fly away. Just like the Beatles song said. I brought a few things to my new place. My new space. Just a few things, but mainly my beautiful (It think) clothes freed from the encasements to protect from their long storage." I remember it was another beautiful day.

Sometimes after three on a Monday afternoon, the 20th day of August 2018. Emptied the corner cabinet that was filled mostly with boxes of photos and albums-- memorabilia keepsakes of cards, notes and letters. Going back in time through memory lane. Monica's trip to Europe after her graduation the little notes she had written. I thought my heart was filled to the brim. Then I found a note from my mother in law. She was like a mother to me. She rarely wrote letters or notes. She was busy, but really, "just not her style." So, this was special. I felt the same for her. We were always close. I felt such a deep sorrow. I still miss her so.

Boy, moving is tough in so many ways. What we find and discover is so unexpected. Are these life lessons reminding us once more, the fleeting of time, the depth of feelings emerges, the joys, the heartaches. What's the purpose? Moving forward gracefully. Wouldn't that be nice, at least easier? Appreciation of that time or these moments. Treasured. Can not be forgotten. I packed my photos, journals, letters, notes and cards carefully. They are precious to me. Why do I feel so deeply? Is it because

I really haven't had the time to process and understand? I don't know. Maybe I should let the tears come. Maybe that is why I feel so weary. Certainly not the fact that my world is non-stop. One of these days, Paul K. is coming to fix the icemaker in my refrigerator—the freezer part. So, I will leave memory lane and focus on the practical and pragmatic part of life. This is what I had written on that Monday afternoon. But this morning I woke up to dark clouds. Then big drops of rain fell straight down from the skies. It really was quite remarkable and mesmerizing too. As I'm standing under protective part of my balcony feeling I'm closer to the end. The end of this writing and I want to make sure that it is worth all the time and energy and is not lost in the shuffle of life. The rain feels cleansing to me reminding me of the thoughts in my head as I awoke early this morning. Actually, these the were words. "It is far greater to feel. Then not to feel at all—ever." Our feeling should never be denied. That is one on the gifts given, is our feelings.

When I was volunteering at the Nursey Crisis Center when the little ones were napping that is when the volunteers would pick up, clean up and reorganize the play area. I was organizing the children's books, when I picked up a book about the importance of feelings. All feelings. And why they are all necessary in life. To pay attention to what our body is telling us. To feel the emotions or know the signs to recognize what is happening to us and around us, to be able to express and understand what makes us happy or sad, angry or excited. Even are senses of being hungry, thirsty, sleepy or sick to our stomach. We have limitation and tolerances.

Our feelings are a gauge telling us and others how our experiences affect us. When we are happy or sad, tired or restless. When we are hurt or angry there is a reason. Sometimes obvious, other times deep seeded. These lessons are taught at a very early age. But we shouldn't stop there in this land of disconnect of the unreachable. These are simple but very valuable tools in life for discernment. Combining our senses with intellect we can form better judgments. We all could benefit when we take time to really listen, see and observe for understanding. Then talk about it, talk about it until there the glimmer of truths and a clearer picture not distorted or fragmented. Then finding and knowing the solutions are there. Now be strong enough and brave enough to face the problems fearlessly. Address and correct. Never accept acts of injustice or inequity. That is our reality to achieve our goals that promote a quality of life for the better. That can happen when we work together. But how do our actions and those transactions that are not so transparent affect us all? There is more to making honey than just money.

chapter 13
MISTY RAINS

Going back to my journal, I had written on September 16th 2018. "I hear softly the church bells ringing in the short distance from Our Lady of Grace. The church where I had taught C.C.D. for nine years and where my family would go to church. I have moved from my little cottage house the 24th of July. I moved when my house was still unsold. In this time, there has been a series of the most unexpected and unknown. The ups and downs of incredible experiences—emotional and physical. I do try to stay in the positive. Knowing there is always a reason and purpose. But I also have met through these past weeks the most amazing and incredible people." It would have been nice to be prepared, forewarned of the consequences of acceptance. And, for whose purpose on all side? But that is not the way things are done any longer. But I have heard of tales once upon a time but I thought we would have learned by now. We should have.

September 28th 2018-- I have sold my house to a wonderful couple. The closing will be the 19th of October. In some ways this will give me some time to process and prepare for the changes ahead. My little cottage house was filled with inspiration inside and out, the nooks and crannies. The large windows filled the rooms with the wonderous natural lighting that inspired not only creativity but softened the tone, the mood and brightened the spirits. There was even a skylight in the kitchen. I appreciated that. It is the unexpected and pleasing touch, giving thought throughout that brought me here. Even going up the stairs led to small skylight, seemingly larger because the mirrors on the sides reflected the light from the skies. Whatever the element, sunshine to misty or rainy days forever providing ambiance. All the rooms were small, with built-in drawers, storage even to the top down desks. So Quaint.

I grew to love that little house. With the beautiful gardens, little pond to explore, work and play, expand the horizon and imagination too. Leading to creating a wonderful little fairy garden that grew through the years. For the kids to play and use their imagination. As they grew older to their amusement. The perfect location to grow moss. Even learned to harvest the moss, for squirrels liked to dig into as they search for their stash of fallen acorns and seeds to horde for the winter. Those pesky squirrels as cute as they were would make a mess digging up my moss. The wonderful thing is, I learned to harvest the moss that grew between the bricks. Naturally grown from nature at it's finest. Serving a dual purpose. Thinning out the moss between the bricks in the patio and walkways would be useful to repair the holes left by the pesky squirrel on the mound of moss for the fairy garden. Repair and replace

But before I moved. I added ambiance lighting outside, in the front and going into the back yard. Accenting the gardens and the lay of the land to enjoy throughout the seasons. Again, to add to the ambiance. Seemed to extend the summer, spring, and fall. And now making the winter evenings more romantic and magical. And just a few months before I moved, while I was at Sunnyside Gardens I saw a most magnificent slender type of fir tree. It was an angel tree. It was beautiful, I could envision it in the south east corner in the front side of my house. It would be symbolic of peace and love for this wonderful cottage and neighborhood too. I would tell everyone of my desire to have an angel tree. They would smile and agree. Would be nice. It would be out of necessity too. For I had some overgrown arborvitae that had to be removed.

I happened to be talking to Billy, who would help me when unexpected projects popped up. And, of course they would always. For nature is unpredictable. I was telling him about the angel tree. He was interested. For he liked to be inspired also. He liked bringing his ideas or any great idea to fruition. Because I had already spent more than I normally would, between my lighting and the removal of the overgrown arborvitaes he suggested we go to Tangle Town for comparison. Not far. On Nicolet and 56th street. Now I like creative ideas, places and possibilities that can be achieved, gracefully and gratefully. It's just a small corner place that offers so much variety and inspiration. Not an inch of space wasted. And it is like tangled town and with tangled brick streets. Really my senses were so heightened, almost overwhelmed. But, would they have an angel tree? I didn't want to get my hopes up. Going around to the back, Billy spots a grove of trees with a few angel trees dispersed within. They were smaller than the one at Sunnyside so for me, more affordable. A baby angel tree, that will grow up with the new owners. It was a little bit taller than me. So, it would be a toddler tree. Not quite a baby. I bought it. Carefully put it in my truck. It's really not a truck, but it's a truck to me.

To this day, I can't believe we actually found a perfect angel tree that fills and fits this space in time. We had to find the perfect location in that corner which was not so easy as there were roots from the past and would there be too much sun or not enough sun? Would the winters be too harsh this year, because I might not be there to protect? Because the summer days were waning, this new little tree would need the right amount of water. So, another big responsibility. If I moved and not be here-- I would have to put my faith in mother nature and the higher power. Mightier than we. Billy did work diligently. Digging the perfectly sized hole to fit. And patting the earth down, protectively with assurance this little tree would grow to be. A few neighbors stopped over to check it all out. Some of my neighbors knew I might be moving. So many mixed emotions. Was I ready to release my keys and leave behind my very creative place that made its' way to my heart? Wasn't easy for any of us.

It is October 3rd, 2018 and I'm getting settled in my condo way of living. I haven't sold my house yet. But, after my last showing with Jeanne and Art, seemed that they were drawn to my house as much as I. It was toward the end of summer. They were to come to see my little cottage one more time. I was not to be there, but there were threats of a bad storm coming. When I talked to Therese, we decided it was better to stay put. She was in the area, so for sure she would be here. She was just a few minutes late. I've always found a good thunderstorm rather exciting. By the time Therese arrived, the weather seemed less foreboding. The energy felt good. When Jeannie and Art arrived, it was just a gentle rain. We are watching as they get out of their car. They both were coming from their work downtown. Jeanne came in. She had a faint smile as if a hard day at the office. Art pretty much lingered outside, enjoying the feel of the gentle warm rain. As if refreshing from his day at the office.

Therese and I greeted Jeanne. I offered her something to drink. Minneapolis does have excellent water. She wanted to see the upstairs once more. I could understand for it was the kind of day that you crave something cozy. I went to check on Art who spotted me at the door. He had this smile on his face of ease and satisfaction. "I knew an artist had to live here." He tells me as he walks in. Introduces himself and looks around. "Well with a name like Art you must be an artist yourself." I tell him. Just some light bantering to ease the stress of it all. He tells me, he's not. But his mother is. But she didn't know she could paint until she moved here in the states. Took her first painting class at age fifty something. She had a natural gift never been tapped until the later stage of her life. What a wonderful gift and inspiration to others. Especially her family.

116

Jeanne and Therese came down the stairs. I could see the faint look of fatigue on her face. "Jeanne why don't you come and sit down for a few minutes?" I tell her. She breathed a sigh of relief as if from a long hard day and finally she could relax. We talked quietly. "Patti, if we buy this house. Could you help me with decorating and the gardening?" I didn't know if she said if or when. I was listening intently for I knew she was so tired. And sometimes just repeating makes you more tired. I think we had a mutual understanding as she is starting to relax. She looks around as if seeing the sunporch for the first time. "Oh Art" She exclaims. You have to see this cute little screened in porch. We walk into the porch. The air feeling soft and refreshing. She looks out into the gardens and the little pond. I told her about planting the little angel tree. She smiled faintly. As we are talking, she's asking me about specific plants. At this time the rains have changed to a very gentle mist. As I am trying to describe to her certain plants, I told her I would just show her.

My shoes are off. I'm already barefoot. I start to go out in the misty rain. "Wait" Jeanne tells me. I'll come outside too". There we were. The misty rain falling gently on our heads. This seemed like the perfect time to tell her about the moss in the fairy garden. I show her the mound of thick moss. And, "look" as I step on top of the mossy area. "You can even walk on this moss. It's so soft on your feet." "let me see." She tells me like a kid once more." "you are right this is soft. This is better than carpet." Yes, it is I tell her. Therese and Art are watching from the screen porch. They both had big grins on their faces. Then Art exclaims as he is taking off his socks. "Wait a minute. You girls are having too much fun. I'm coming out to test that moss. And, he did. We are all gently laughing barefoot in the misty rain. At that moment we were grownups being kids once more. In this magical place on a rainy day, amidst all the serious business matters at hand. It is times like this that we hold on to. The wonder and magic of it all. Embracing the moment and just be free.

I knew then, that my little cottage house would be sold. To this very wonderful couple. That did make it easier for me to let go. And let be. Still was not easy. I cherished that time. All the challenges that taught me how. How to do, when I didn't know I could. For that I am grateful. I think back at my little cottage house, I felt I was of the earth. A part of. Depending on me. Yet it nourished and comforted me in return.

117

Small sculptured bunny tiny baby tears spilling over

Discovering mother nature. All the wonders of the seasons. The long cold winter. What possibly can survive it all. Spring comes and this little forgotten bunny planter lost in the leaves and then the snow. Would wake up to the warmth of spring with tiny little leaves spilling to the ground. It is like a treasure. Thank God for teaching mother nature so well. Now teach me. Teach us all.

chapter 14

A LITTLE CROOKED–
MAYBE

It seems to me that this would be the perfect ending of this book. I would like that. The perfect ending. Yet, there was so much more to this experience than to let slip into the land of forgetfulness. There would be a closing of my little cottage house. Seemed the date would be changed from the 19th to finally settling on the 12th of October. The time too, would change from 5:00 pm to 11:00 am then finally to accommodate 9:00 am would work the best. Therese told me I didn't necessarily have to be there. But I told her I had to be there. I wanted to hand over the keys myself. Sitting at the long table were a panel of women and one man. About six in all. They were all gracious as I walked in the room. I tried to memorize their names, after all the introductions were formalized. There was such a tone of gentleness almost as a family gathering. Guiding the way of certainty.

Now this transaction could be started and finalized. They all had their own separate role or part which they would state their position, their purpose and any questions please to be answered. This must have been the time and place, but I was almost mesmerized by the reality of the whole experience. I know part of this feeling was mixed for myself, plus the sheer fact that I was coming through that long illness. Toward the end, Dan, the lone solitary kind man from the bank that I was now using, explained the dynamics of my payments, and was assuring me that he was providing the best outcome for me. And, that I know he did. For he seemed to know what I had been through and wanted to make this transaction work for me. This business at hand was now concluded. Winding down, our conversation was light with hopes and promise. I handed my keys to Jeanne and Art along with my note I had written of gratitude and goodwill. "Patti, we have a little something for you too." I opened the little box to find a pretty little bowl to hold my treasures. "It was hand made in Poland" Art proudly told me. This little bowl of porcelain / ceramic with colors of blue flowers with a touch of yellow, with leafy greens against the white backdrop. Filigree style. A beautiful keepsake with a story to be told.

Shortly after that, I had a question that I felt important. But I learned that they had changed things around at my new bank. And, Dan was no longer working there. How could this have happened so quickly? This brought back memories of my former bank, when the staff could be moved around. One day here. The next day gone. I didn't like that feeling of uncertainty. Just when establishing a trusting business relationship, there would be a relocation. I felt it was part of the disconnect. A control on big businesses part. I'm not sure if that is such a good thing?

120   During this time and even before. I would see and hear about the financial struggles of those around me. In fact, many times in desperation they would reach out to me for assistance of some kind. Maybe just to help them get through the week, the month. Maybe some groceries would help. If behind in their bills—just enough to get them through. And then, help with their house payment or their rent. It was like a revolving door. So many, so much what is going on? I'm not a bank and certainly not an ATM machine. Aren't the banks purpose is to provide when times are down?

Where is all our tax dollars going to, if not to provide? But not anymore. Their main concern is acquiring and maintaining their own wealth. The interest is for the monetary growth for themselves. Credit cards will be their answer. Get them when they're weak and weary and a desperate state of mind and being. We can make a nice profit in these times of desperation. So, what if they are inexperienced, this will be their time to learn their lessons the hard way. School of hard knocks. Those who are / were in position to help now were no longer available. Refusing, yet continued to profit from services these people gave until needed no longer. Using the money from the losses of others, without a thought or care. While their pockets and banking accounts are overflowing. Or tightly hidden in view from the internal revenue. I've said enough about this. About this problem that has continued for years and never addressed. Now I will continue why I'm rather upset and still a bit perplexed. Questions needing answers.

I would move from my little cottage house, for how long I would not know. I would now be making two mortgage payments plus double utility bills and always the unexpected. Left me with little in return. It doesn't take a rocket scientist, or mathematician or most noted scholar to know or realize there is something a bit off, a little crooked maybe, needs to be straightened, adjusted put in the right alignment whatever corrections needed to be applied. Mistakes need to be attended and brought to the attention in order not to create more havoc, more problems and eventually erosion of our quality of life.

121

The inequity or inequality keeps getting bigger, more noticeable Yet, no one addresses the obvious disparity or question the cause and effect. They know it. And see and feel it but they never address it, until it fits their agenda. Then it becomes a hot topic. But not discussed until their profit is made. At this stage in life, shouldn't we all be smarter, wiser, more aware, more understanding leading to being more benevolent? But we still believe that money is the solution to everything. Unbelievable. We are supposed to live and learn. Not to repeat the same mistakes over and over again, in our quest for more affluence, that will influence the outcome. Not what we thought? Not what we were led to believe? Are we willing to sacrifice others? Well, we know the answer to that question.

When we are in the midst of these occurrences it does affect us all. If we have heart, we understand our feelings or emotions. We will feel their pain, their suffering and understand their struggle. When we love money, the acquiring of more, usually for ourselves, sometimes for our family and it's really nice what all that money can provide and hide and look how the masses-- that money impresses. Forgetting those who live in a state of constant financial desperation, become desperate. That state of mind or being leads to bigger problems. For their plight serves no good purpose. To be held down or back. Yuk, I don't want to write about this, but now the table has turned. And, I have looked at the picture. And it's not pretty. Just pretty pathetic, maybe prophetic too. It's sad even discouraging for, I know we can do better than this. Can't we see what needs to be addressed? Hear what the problems are. And bring solutions to the table that inspire everyone. From the brightest to the darkened mind finally brought to the light. But what I have noticed or experienced is how easily we can accept when dependent on that check. Is that the reason it is easier to comply, give up and give in forgetting our moral conscience or scruples in the process. Until, we can no longer remember what is right or what is just plain wrong. Do we want to go down that rocky road again?

Years before I even moved into my little cottage, it would be the banks, financial institutions, professionals that had their own best interest at heart and would be my nemesis and many others too. Especially after the economic crash in 2008. Of course, with the help of our big government, the banks and financial institutions would be bailed out They became wealthier than ever while we continue playing catch up to this day. The rules were changed to protect their best interest. While the majority paid the price of their recklessness and carelessness in each new venture. We learned not to trust. And they learned it was okay and acceptable to take--from others. Their rewards would be great but would never learn from their mistakes. Perpetuate problems and profit from them too. They never deserved when taking from those who served. The games people play. Yet, we keep playing. Thinking, one day the rules soon will be fair and just. But some command and demand special privileges no matter how glaring to serve them well. When is there restitution to be paid, instead of homage? That is misconstrued.

Buddha Cat

Buddha Cat is what I call him. Welcoming at the door with a pleasant disposition. He's a pretty wise judge of character. So, when people who come to the door, they are automatically at their best behavior. They want to bring out the best part of them self. And vice versa. For Buddha Cat is a reminder of grace and gratitude. Kindness and service. Bringing a sense of respect and dignity in the moment. Whatever is asked of you, do willingly and joyfully. Smile a little, a little bit more, be thankful and blessings will follow.

Guard Cat

Guard Cat is so alert. He observes everything and everyone. He is quite discerning taking his job so seriously that impresses everyone. So, it seems once again most people are on their best behavior. But there have been moments that was a bit unsettling for this big guy. When all those arborvitae trees had to be removed. Now the sun was too harsh for him. The wind a little too strong. He felt a little vulnerable at this time. Until, we were sure to plant his favorite flowers, he loves moss roses. And, we bought him an Angel Tree to help keep him company. He really liked that. He was filled with gratitude. Now instead of being sad and slightly mad, he became a happy camper once more doing his job. Well done.

Boulevard Garden & a Touch of Wonder

This is the tree in the boulevard, where I put a little fairy land around on the trunk of the tree. To add a little more whimsy for the children and childlike in this wonderful little neighborhood."

chapter 15

A Blast of Cold Air and Warmth of Loving Care

I don't mean to repeat these acts, actions and transactions experiences, I just want a clearer understanding of responsibility and consequences. Wouldn't those in these specialized positions take notice, take heed and question the numbers put in and the numbers going out? Was this typical or was this a deliberate outcome put in place? Was this contract designed specifically for an unknown reason or to further that hidden agenda? That only a few would be privy to know, understand but also benefit. Another added incentive. An artificial means that maintains that status or the status quo. Only a manmade idea designed to guarantee and further control a desired result at the conclusion of transactions. Some more than others. Now this is serious and should be understood by everyone. For the consequences are played out for years. Affecting not only oneself, but a widespread practice put in place deliberately to protect and ensure the wealth of those who have gone beyond. As an addiction out of control. What are we to do? How do we address this fact? Or even approach these facts when beginning at the top? They should be aware of what they approve.

This I do know, when treated well we respond well. I had written this in my journal October 19, 2018. In this time, the most challenging experiences wrapped up in one. One for the books. Got through them all, even though somewhat bewildered. Still presented a greater understanding and realization almost as an epiphany. But what was I to do and do I address? I just know, there are too many man-made problems meant for what reason. We can only surmise. In this period of disconnect created uncertainty and doubt. Transactions vague. More red tape than needed or necessary. We should all wonder. Expecting a brilliant epiphany. Finding the most humble and sincere actions speaks volumes. The importance of simplicity, trusting out instincts, knowing our purpose and setting our goals-- leads to determination, action and independence. Having the key that unlocks the door to enlightenment. Knowing we are able, we have arrived and survived the stresses. Free of the man-made obstacles meant to weaken our resolve even to doubt ourselves.

When, what we need is a change in our direction, our thinking. Focusing more on our attributes that is constructive not harmful or destructive. Not insidiously or deliberately finding ways erode or use or misuse funds to benefit oneself, corporation or another avenue for the banks to gain once again more than their share or more than their worth. It is time we wake up to what is going on around us. Question the rationale of such documentation or transactions that are vague or misleading. Then ascertain using sound judgment without a conflict of interest. Is it dependable and reliable serving the real purpose or intent? Or will this contract have a degrading or eroding factor? Or will that product heal or lead to an addiction of another kind, hurting the body and destroying the mind insidiously in the process. Have these transactions and products become acceptable for the thrill of the risks, taking a chance but also profitable in the process?

128

Wait a minute. Am I projecting too many areas into this topic? Yes. I am. Because they are all related. There needs to be a reason when there if no longer sound judgement. Is it because of an exhausted state of being? Or has it become darker than just needing a break? Has it become a hard habit to break? Like one too many cocktails, maybe? Helps to relax. Or get through the day. It's socially acceptable you know to have that cocktail hour, where we can discuss business matters. Maybe, a little cloudy but lessens the inhibitions. No one can stop us now. Reckless and daring with your money, your life, as well as the quality of life of others. It's all a blur.

And those little pills for every imaginable ailment or every neurotic condition even if temporary. Once again depending on a pill to get you through the night or even through the day without a hint of anxiety, stress or nervousness. Remember those strong feelings or emotions are telling our body and our mind there is something amiss. Listen to your instincts. They are trying to tell you what is needed or not necessary. That takes a certain amount of trust in yourself. Knowing your strengths and your own weakness and limitation. But we are led to believe we are not capable. We are not the expert or the professional in this area. But are they?

When their judgment might be eschewed from one too many. Or based on the bottom line or the revenue that becomes high stakes for themselves now their main objective and purpose. Blocked, blinded and indifferent and inconsiderate from their greed. Incapable of recognizing their own part in the chaos around. Sometimes the seeming easy way is the most detrimental. For we haven't trusted enough to stand up against big money. We are still so impressed. We do nothing. We acquiesce. We trust. We accept. We take that little drink to soften the conscience. We take that little pill to get us through the day. Walking zombies. Is that what is wanted. Can't we talk it through or walk it out or remove the source of angst or problem or just plain figure it out. What is the problem? There are times, I guess we could use that pill. But we have become over medicated, over prescribed to the point of addiction, dependency on that little pill, blue, green, pink or yellow, red or white. All so pretty. Looks harmless. Combine it with that small glass wine. Isn't that what we are not supposed to do? But once deluded it doesn't matter-- if it does or doesn't make things right. I do have my concerns about these documentations. What they teach us and where they lead us.

129

Everyone doing their job, doing what they are paid to do. Have they noticed the changes though the years or are they new and inexperienced and have nothing to compare? No guide lines. When I was signing all the papers for my closing as wonderful as everyone was and how I so much wanted to believe that this was in everyone's best interest. I felt certainly for me, for one thing I was coming from that long illness. So, physically I felt vulnerable. Not at my best. Yet because of that state, I felt as if in a state of grace. I was still here. I was still capable. But, did I recognize what was really happening? Should I have accepted? Shouldn't I at least have questioned? Maybe, I was weary but thankful that I would not be paying two of everything. But "after all was said and done" and I received the check after the closing. I was stymied, perplexed seeing the amount.

How could this be when I bought this house for 470,000 dollars. The problems were never disclosed. Even when I contacted Edina Realty and told them about all the problems. I was told they were working on it. I had written about this part in my second book. But I did feel that because I addressed this immediately something would be done. Maybe a reimbursement settlement for the non-disclosed problems needing repaired to even buying this house back from me. Days turned into week, then months and years. Nothing was ever done. My calls were never answered and if they were—they were so busy they would have to call me back. I wrote numerous letters. All to no avail. I had bought this little house in October of 2006. It was a very challenging time for me, for I had learned Merrill Lynch had taken the sale of my original house I sold—without my knowledge or consent invested that money and lost it all. Plus, the money I had for my future financial security would be used also, and they lost most of that money too. Leaving me with barely 200,000. They had lost almost 800,000 dollars leaving me dependent on money I receive each month.

I would end up living in my little cottage house for almost twelve years. Every month, I would pay on the principle for that is what I was told to do. Now I have very little extra money to put back then--but I did. I put that extra fifty dollars, hundred or more, occasionally 250, 300 even four hundred dollars to add to my house payment every month. Well after twelve years that adds up to a respectable sum of money. Not the money that Merrill Lynch had used and lost, but it was interesting to see how the payment reflected on the cost of my house. That inspired me and gave me the impetus to add more to the principle. That should count for something. On top of that I had put well over 200,000 dollars into the repair and restoration of my little cottage. I had written about that also. So, I lived there from October of 2006 and sold my little cottage in October of 2018. Are you good at math? Well it's not my area of expertise but I am relatively better than you think I am and better than I want to be. For it's not my favorite thing—the numbers. The numbers game. Should be ashamed. Now, I'm getting delirious for "to me this is tedious" not what I want to talk about, write about. It just makes me perturbed or sleepy. Depending on the time of day, sometime that doesn't matter either or the reason why this "has to be" the topic.

The realty of my situation sinks in. It was bad enough that I put well over 200,000 dollars in my house that I paid too much for. But, to sell it for the same price that I bought it for was ludicrous. Just too bizarre. Even close to sinister. For what purpose? What was the motive? I even paid on the principle for all those years. Who got that money? To whom and where did that money go? I had less money now to put on my new place. That had never happened before. The real estate world was using the housing market the same way the big banks and corporate America would use and abuse the trust of the people. For their profit only. With the cooperation with big government, wall street the big banks too. They would not fail. For everyone needs a home. Redesigned contracts, with designer rules and laws put in place guaranteed their successes.

Because of my meager cost of living every two years, I would be spared. But now, I was in an emotional quandary.

The cause and effect of the dysfunction and corruption for all these years, was creating desperation in all areas. Those who lost were trying to survive. The hardships for their families was unthinkable and unbearable. They had nowhere to turn to for financial aid or help. For the banks didn't learn anything from the financial crash. Except to find ways to profit themselves. It wasn't in their best interest to delve a little deeper into the cause and effect. How this happened in the first place? Why was this allowed? For whose purpose? This could have been a simple fix. But then they

131

would not be able to test and apply their reckless endeavors. First, they would make sure their coffers were filled to the brim. Before their reckless plans were exposed. It was easy for them in this time of disconnect. Underhanded deals made without a thought or care for those who were caught in their web of deception. The glory years of dysfunction. Benefits without merit.

I worried for those who sold their house to the bank. In desperation, I knew those who fell into that hook, line and sinker. I worried for those who were told to just go bankrupt. And, eventually they did. They tried every avenue they could think of until they just bit the bullet and did just that. It was a traumatic experience for all. And, feeling helpless when there was very little I could do to help. I remember a dear friend of mine, trustingly took on a five-year loan. She was planning on moving within that time. But, those five years flew by. Her house not sold. The five years of plenty was up. The bank couldn't wait to raise her rates to more than double her previous mortgage payments. Now unaffordable. Creating tremendous hardships. There were no boundaries for the seekers of properties to sell or buy. Even buy as an investment, for they were one of the lucky ones who made a certain amount of profit from the collapse. It would be interesting to learn or know what went on behind the scene. During this time.

For me, now that my house was sold gave me a certain relief. Yet, what was happening to those around me was confusing also. I was puzzled by the series of events that kept leading to a control that was beyond reasoning. I knew it was creating a huge disparity. For those in control, in the know would continually profit. Even when it was all over. Said and done. Meanwhile, not a thought or care to those who lost their home, their financial security, even their livelihood was taken right from under. I could not help but feel a growing anger to those who had caused and profited. Not only profited but was rewarded. Became wealthier than ever. Off the backs of their predecessors. We have become a merciless country where the profit gained is more important than the quality of life left behind. Sacrificing the best, all for the love of more. But, it's an empty lonely life. For you live with yourself with the misdeeds of the past that is too painful to breach. How could this happen? How can you hurt your own?

I'm sorry. This is just so difficult to write about. For there were many innocent people who simply didn't know. Their lives filled to the brim. Not with money. But financial debts left behind, growing larger for inflation and taxes were always greater than the income coming in. Sometimes they blamed themselves. For they listened to the best. They trusted those in position. Only to lose everything. And now, would also pay the price for those who caused. While those who caused benefitted. Profited. Never having to give back. How could people be so controlled? When I hear a financier asking the question, "why aren't people saving their money?" When the question should be for, "those who caused the collapse—why didn't they have to give back?" Is he serious? Hasn't he heard of being responsible, accountable when caught and restitution to be paid for those who suffered great loss. What is missing here? We are going backwards. The dumbing of our country. All because of recklessness, carelessness rewarded. Never having to face the truths or consequences of their deceptive practices. Isn't it time we face the truths and right the wrongs?

Although my house was sold, Jeanne and Art still had their family home to sell. They wanted to downsize and live closer to the city for commuting purpose. Their plans were to move after their last child was to graduate. So, like myself they would have double everything. Mine fortunately was temporary. But at least they could take time and plan. They pretty much knew what to expect, but the unexpected always appears. Either in the form of mother nature or those from the rise and "hardly ever" the fall or the call of taxes and expenses.

I only have a few pages left in my journal. If they are relevant, I will continue to use excerpts for percipience. Written the twelfth day of December 2018. Still so much to do. Experiences from the past come back to me as a blast of cold air, forcing issues that were never laid to rest. And will continue to come back until finally attended. Are there solutions to be found? I believe so. But only if the ego allows. I am to go see my new tax man. Between my long illness and selling my house there will be plenty to discuss and catch upon. That is enough I will say about the subject of taxes. Through all these years of paying quarterly taxes. I had enough. I finally was bold enough, strong enough and had enough.

I put my foot down. Wrote various letters about this topic and sent to the big and small government. "No more quarterly taxes. I'm going to pay my taxes once a year, like everybody else! So, this meeting with Jim L. was to seal the deal. I don't like that expression. But for what I have been through and so many others that was as good as it gets. And they should be thankful. Thank their lucky stars, that they haven't been thrown off their perch. Jim did tell me, "once I paid off that hefty some of money. I was too weak to pay when I was so ill. Missed a couple of payments in my delirium and it grew. Horrible experience in both accounts. At least, I would no longer have to pay quarterly taxes." It's about time. How could anyone or any organization care more about the books "I mean the numbers kind" than about a human life? Is beyond my comprehension. No more quarterly taxes!

December 13, 2018. I had to stop my writing. My rambling. I'm feeling tired. Too much is going on in unsettled space. My head is in a whirl. Where do I begin? What do I do first? I think meeting my tax man Jim wore me out, just getting there. At least this time I didn't get lost. I also wrote another check for a huge sum of money. This was a follow up meeting from yesterday. "Maintenant de nos jours-- complet; or compléter" in French. Maybe my next book will be in French.

"This little cottage house had it all even a little man made pond surrounded by stone. An added delight or project to take care even redesign. Seemed someone always wanted to rearrange something. I would have Koi (little fish) placed in the pond late spring early summer. Depending on the weather. When the weather would change to cooler temps would have the Koi removed back to their safety and warmth."

chapter 16
PRECIPITATION

Now we are in the month of January the 30th 2019. What I've experienced as well as many others. I just write about it. To be known. To not repeat the same mistakes or allow others to be reckless because of their status. Enough of that. They would feel better about themselves if they were held accountable and had to be responsible instead of becoming glorified rogues living in ostentatious splendor. Subconsciously, they feel that deep rooted shame. But who are they to blame? They could stand up and admit their mistakes or nefarious actions too painful to bare. But that takes a very big man. A strong man of character. That could be their goal, their mission to change themselves into being admirable. Trustworthy and compassionate. Person of integrity and honor. Civility at it's finest for others to follow or aspire. Change their way and still be paid. Just enough to experience another way. Not so daring. But of sharing. Instead of acquiring try hiring. Learn a new skill one that builds. Confidence with compliments. Constructive instead of destructive. Help each other. Your sister, your brother. Try a new way, a better way and take time to enjoy the day.

We are in January. Might as well experience the cold. The chill in the air that gives you the shivers. So much so you dress in layers. The cold will take your mind off all those struggles. Those experiences that were meant to break will be replaced by determination not to give up or give in. For what reason or purpose. Usually its for someone's profit. Now it's for sheer survival. It all hits home. The reality, the deception, the ongoing plan without consequences. Is it learned as if a game, a game of chess? Or is it as a graceful dance to distract from the pact. The pact of silence of what we can no longer bare or share. It is the cold winter that brings the despair.

Not the past that we don't want to hear. Or remember. It's okay we all make mistakes. We can forgive and forget in sincerity of repair. Mend the broken heart. Heal the body. Comfort the lost soul. Give peace to inspire the mind. For the lasting good of all.

The January of 2018 introduced us to record breaking cold and winds with temperatures well below zero. Day and night. The post office was even closed today. Along with everything else. Pipes freezing, cars and trucks too. Creating a mess. Scary too. Don't want to be stranded out there. I can see it all from the safety of my balcony. It's a weird feeling being in this condo. Somewhat protected from the ferocity of the elements. Yet, the effects seem more daunting in a psychological way than the physical. I'm removed from it all. I do miss my little cottage house. But this winters' cold. I wonder If I could have survived it all, I don't know. If Arman was here, we would bundle up and explore the elements. Not too far. Just to have the experience.

This morning Andre called from New York and we finished the revision of my first book. It took several hours. Afterwards, I felt exhausted. Yet a sense of relief and a release, for so long I knew the revision was necessary. Because it was so cold. I was dressed in my warmest and comfortable layers. In fact, while working, halfway through was so hot I had to remove my warm socks. Pulled off my now overly warm sweater and put my hair up off my neck. That helped. And continued until we finished our work. After we finished going through all those pages I felt totally drained. While leafing through my worn pages studying the contents. I became chilled. I was in such deep concentration it wasn't until then would I realize, how unusually cold I was. I put my warm socks back on. Pulled my hair down and put my warmest sweater back on over all my layers. I was freezing cold. But hungry too. I still had half of my grilled cheese sandwich I had made yesterday. Heated up my leftover cup of tomato soup about a quarter of one and had my lunch. A very productive morning.

Had a call from Paul K. His truck was frozen and would not be able to get here to install the rest of my lighting today. Those lights were to go in the kitchen and dining area. That was not such a good thing for me, but in retrospect turned out to be the best thing for me. For it did give me a break, a needed respite and time to gather my thoughts for my next book. This would be my last book that I would write of such serious nature. For I said after this, I would do an art book. A book of my paintings, a book to inspire the latent or budding new artist. All that is needed is a little nudge, a few supplies a quiet space even a lively space to create. Acknowledgment is important so an occasional whisper of praise in awe that inspires and encourages the love of the arts and the value of creativity. Enhancing for life. Add a couple of children's books to the mix. These long winters are a writer's haven. In fact, all the seasons offer an incredible opportunity It's amazing what hidden talents are concealed beneath the surface just waiting to burst forth or quietly unfold. Our talent and abilities are our gifts to be used to inspire and use for the good of all.

139

Tomorrow I am to see Dr. Hu, my acupuncturist. I haven't been feeling right. For one thing, my appetite has been waning. The fatigue is a nuisance when there are things I want to do. Yet this has been going on for a while. I need to listen to what my body is telling me. So, I try to be more aware and take care. Fore. I want to be in the moment. Not all over the place. The only thing is, I will have to call to make sure the office will be open because of the severe cold and conditions. The weather has been so bizarre. In these past few months, "it's like this door, slightly ajar, slightly open letting in memories. The past has presented many obstacles. Yet soon will be the promise of better times. But we all need to do our part to achieve this. For we can't do it alone." The temperature will be going down to 27 degrees below zero…

"And it did. We woke up to 27 degrees below zero. That's cold enough. We don't need to break anymore records. It is eerily cold. It is 7:30 in the morning, the sun is faint from the cold. As if, far as possible to shield from the freezing air. Yet, not so far that we forget. There will be better days

In my journal it is Monday February 4th 2019 a beautiful day. Adriana and the girls Melissa and Jenna are coming over. I greeted them at the door in the main level of the lobby. When the girls saw me. They are both enthusiastic and energetic as I greet them. They are jumping up and down with big smiles on their little face. Made my day. Guess how old we are now Momé? Before I could think of a magical number, they both say in chorus. "I'm seven and I'm five." "That is impossible. How could that be?" I tell them. They laughed and giggled as if a great joke played. We all went up the magical elevator to #416 to see and explore my new digs.

Children have such enthusiasm and curiosity. I love it. I pulled the big soft white, shaggy rug with a big heart in the center. The heart deep shade of pink to place on the floor in the living room. That looked out on to the balcony. So cozy and inviting. They sat on the floor with their little lamb and bunny, I had bought for them. Along with my Teddy Von Maur bear wearing his best and only plaid pajamas. We called him Teddy Von Maur. There they were, at play using their imaginations as they shared their treats with little lamb, bunny and baby bear, happily sitting on the rug with the big pink heart. Sharing their snacks and drinking their water through a straw. There interaction with each other is warming to watch.

A wonderful way to wind down is with books or writing little notes. I happened to be at the small Barnes and Noble Book Store off Excelsior and Lake Street when I found a book Mary Bella's Missing Valentines—a story book for children. Since it was soon to be Valentine Day, I wanted Adriana and the girls over to play. I told her about the book that I was drawn to for my sister's name is Mary Belle. Sometimes we call her Mary Bella for when Vince was little that is what he would call my sister. Melissa and Jenna both love to draw and color. I had an idea of writing a note and sending it off. I told Adriana and the girls about having the girls write a little note or draw a little picture or just sign their name. And then I would enclose their little notes along with my own note inside the story book. To be sent to my sister all the way to Colorado. Their eyes wide, listening to my directions. They liked that idea.

Melissa since she was two years older was a bit more industrious. Jenna since she was younger became rather quiet. In deep thought. Thinking of this daunting task that lay before her. Can she? And could she? Maybe a little overwhelmed about the whole plan. Melissa wanted to draw a picture of her nummy. My sister had given it to her when she was first born. And she still has it. In fact, her little sister Jenna wanted one just like hers. Jenna carefully printed her name as best she could on her note. Then added different colors with the markers. This was a lot of work for this little one. She was so determined to get it right that she wore herself out. She's doing so well with her condition that I almost forget that her little body is constantly healing. That "in itself" tires her more than most children for she is in a constant state of healing.

When Jenna was born, she was rushed by ambulance to Abbott Children Memorial for there was something seriously wrong. This was so unexpected. No one knew what was wrong, or even if she would live. Several weeks later, and after many tests they would learn she had E.B. She could not be held. She could not be touched. She could not even touch herself. Her skin was so delicate. I wrote about this experience that shook us to the core. And still when I think of that time I'm overwhelmed. At that time not knowing what to expect or how to care for a child that cannot be touched—did not seem possible. My son never left her side. Standing guard over her and on constant alert. At night he slept on the small hard sofa in the room. Not meant for sleeping. He was vigilant in her care. Determined to learn himself how to care for his child. So much so that he would show the new nurses and doctors how to care for her. But even while they were there, he lovingly took over that role. Adriana was not yet fully recovered from her caesarean insisted on leaving the hospital—she needed to see for herself the seriousness of her baby. Her baby needed her presence as much she needed her child. Being in this delicate state and still recovering from shock was not going to hold her back.

One of the most beautiful memories for me, was watching my son so tenderly and lovingly and ever so gently teach Adriana how to care for their baby daughter. For Adriana was still recovering herself. But she was resolute in purpose to learn to heal and take care of her baby. For she is a mother. And nothing was going to keep her from her child. She is listening so intently to her husband as he gently teaches, together." My son Duane never left the hospital. Except when Adriana insisted, he go home. Shower, shave and rest. Then come back. He was the one who initially learned how to care for Jenna's wounds. So that was not easy for him to leave, but he knew he was in an exhausted state. This was good for Adriana too, to feel confident enough and competent too. She was now ready. Still in a fragile state, but her will and perseverance was strong.

That was Jenna's introduction to the world. Now she is five... And, she is a gift to all of us. Coming from a most fragile state requiring diligent 24 hour watch and care. It's amazing how she has endured and accepted her plight. She is a special child with deep concentration and strong determination to do and be. She's such a serious child (of course) but she also has a sense of humor through it all and at times will surprise and test the best of us, especially her big sister. So she's that wonderful, bright and ever precocious child who is a natural wonder and miracle child. One of her favorite things to do is playing with her sister Melissa who helps and teaches her throughout the day. One of her favorite pastimes is to write notes to her friends and cousins and her Aunt Mary Bell-a sending her note all the way to Colorado.

That was a gift on Valentine day that my sister would always remember and cherish. From Minnesota to Colorado. We had such a nice visit. We packed up everything that was needed to go. Including the little Lamb, bunny and Teddy Von Maur. As a gift for baby Tony. I walked them down to the Lobby. And watched as they loaded up their car. We said our sweet good- byes. Maybe this can be a tradition.

Last week, when Paul was to install my lighting, he called once more to tell me his diesel truck was frozen and wouldn't start. Woe is me I'm thinking. I did understand and tried to be gracious in my disappointment. I was also trying to picture everything that had to be done to unfreeze his frozen truck. First of all, I pictured it encased with ice. Then a mix of snow and ice that would have to be removed. To get I believe, that hood of the truck opened to put some kind of heater in. Get the heater started to warm up, to get the motor going. "Get the motor running. Head out to the highway. Looking for adventure. Whatever comes my way." Minnesota is laden with adventures. But, do you remember that song? That song was applicable to the moment.

That was on a Thursday. On Friday afternoon Paul called and said he could put the lights in today. His car was now in working order, but that frozen problem also created a backup. I was finally having the lights put in over the dining room table as a softly lit jewel. He also put the dimmers in. I tell you this man can do anything. Then he put in the two lights in the kitchen which was quite the transformation. Might take some getting used to. But better than before. The one last thing which was the small pendant lighting to go over the sink. Pretty exciting. Long time coming. Except the last thing to put in, the small pendant which should have been a piece of cake. Turned out to be complicated. Just opening up the packaging was tough. But Paul is a patient man as he is unraveling all of the protective coverings of the lighting and the wires. I'm waiting patiently. He pulled out this mass of wires. Which was also a mess. So long and had to be rewound and rethreaded. "Patti, I'm going to have to take this home, as I'm running out of time. But I will finish it at home. I will have more space to spread the wires out. I'll have to do some cutting." He sounded like a surgeon explain the procedure. Is that okay? Sure. What else could I say?

Now would you believe on Super Bowl Sunday. Paul called. I think it was good news, but he always sounds positive. Well, most of the time. He called to tell me he finished working on the drop pendant. "I can come over right now and put it up for you. I didn't like knowing you were without lights in your kitchen." Wow, another great day. When not lit, the glass drop pendant is swirled layers of rusty browns, golds and amber colors. When turned on, the colors really come out. Specs of orange, various shades of amber and rusty tones. Bringing a softness and ambiance to my kitchen. That turned out to be a bigger project than thought. But it was true, I was without lights in my kitchen when Paul left the power in that space had to be closed. A minor inconvenience to me. But how considerate of this man who gives so much of his time. Without a complaint or an agenda. He enjoys his work and that is the key.

I had written on another Thursday the 7th day of February. I was to see Dr. Hu today. Same as last week. I barely got there intact. But I did. The weather has been most challenging, between the extreme cold and the blowing snow, that covers the ice underneath. Sometimes, black ice. Which is even more slick or slippery. But the wind was blowing more than before as if angry or testing everyone. But when I got there, the vestibule was filled with people waiting for a treatment of some kind. I had never seen it this busy before. Now seeing all these people needing and needed, I felt I should reschedule. For I knew there was no way I could relax and have my treatment knowing there were others so much worse. At that moment, I was fine, when I looked around to see. I knew I did the right thing, When Dr.Hu briefly came from her office, I told her it was better for me to reschedule for the following week. I recognized that weariness and knew her commitment. She was grateful and gracious as always. I would see Dr. Hu the following week.

chapter 17

A Wake-Up Call

It was the 14th day of March 2019. So much going on, it was impossible to write except for a few paragraphs about the weather, the busyness and woe is me. Can I get through this day? "It was over a month ago that I had written these few short lines." "Woke up to blue skies. Almost forgot how wonderful the sun can make not only the day, but life does not seem so formidable, giving hope and energy to carry on. Even though it is still extremely cold. The high right now is minus five below zero. Shivers. I will be going out for I have errands to do this afternoon. I have to tread carefully for the hidden ice". That was the last I had written since March. But when having such severity of weather, there will be a cause and effect. The snow and ice will not just miraculously melt away. There is a process in nature that we eventually understand with experience.

When I lived in different states where the weather was more moderate, there would be March winds blow and April showers bring May Flowers. And that can be true, but more likely not in Minnesota. I'm not going to expound on the weather. Just the fact that the winter of 2018 did break all kinds of records. But Minnesotans are a fan of keeping records and likes to be noticed for whatever. The most or the least. It doesn't matter. Just going from winter to spring is not only challenging but also offering the most beautiful spring. The snow melts over the ice. Even on the warmest day be careful of the puddle that hides thin layers of slippery ice. Finally, those warm days appear-- melting of more, or rain that cleans the air and the earth. Will freeze over in the night turning to ice even when it's nice. Leading to a slippery start of the day. So, an abundance of challenges That will energize and inspire the senses specially with anticipation and inspiration for gardening, clearing up, cleaning up bringing possibilities for rearranging the gardens. Natures' way of keeping us alert and aware. To be there and take care.

We had so much precipitation in one form or another. Winter leading into spring. I awoke with the sound of rain. It's around eight in the morning, I could have been disheartened with all the rain that we've had. But I must have been thankful instead. I woke up singing and I told myself I am going to sing this to the kids when they get tired of the rain. Putting everything in perspective. We all know this little song we sang as a child. Sometimes needing to be sung several times. So, it teaches patience, musicality, timing and etiquette. Por favor.

"Rain, rain go away. Come again another day. Rain, rain go away. Go away today." Now this is what I added in my delirium. But with a change of rhythm Like the rhythm of life. "For, we've had enough precipitation. Enough precipitation. Enough precipitation. We've had enough precipitation. Rain please go away. So we can play. Today. Please." Actually, you have to hear it to appreciate it. And to see it to believe it. We had the worst winter and got through it. Now bring on the rain. The beginning of the winter season really was not that bad. But got really cold, with hardly any snow. Toward the end of January—snow and more snow. Had ice on top of the snow. Then a gentle steady rain fell and turned the beautiful mounds of snow, into not like any surface of snow seen before. The mounds of snow now pitted with holes from the rains. It looked like we were on another planet. Snow, rain and smog too. Looked like no season ever recorded. This would also the last winter I would experience in my little cottage house. Magical and mystical.

chapter 18
WHY SHOULD THIS SURPRISE ME?

I had not written again until April 24th of 2019. But there was a reason for this absence. Certainly not expected, but after everything going on around me, it was just a matter of time. In fact, just a little over a month ago, March 13th 2019, I've had a lot going on for so long—becoming a way of life. Accepting   this as normal. Everyone it seemed was stretched to the max. So, I was not alone. I felt because I have always lived such a healthy life, I was almost invincible. But for years I have lived under a cloud of stress from all directions. That would be my downfall. Like too much snow on the roof and roof caves in from the weight of it all. When I had that illness that lasted for over a year-- didn't help.

The ongoing issues that were never addressed continued without a thought from those who were party to. As wonderful as my little cottage was, the noise for me was almost unbearable. It was rare that I had a full night of sleep. I felt I was on sensory overload with no escape. People would say you'll get used to it. I never could. For if anything, they would add more runways. More airplanes. Disregarding the impact to these wonderful neighborhoods. I would go to meetings about this problem. Hundreds of people would speak up, speak out to no avail. They would have meetings about these problems, but nothing was ever done. So nice, seemingly so concerned but nothing was ever done. Was it a big pretense to lead people on, to seal the deals? Distract the masses.

Depending on your district you could have soundproof windows installed for free or minimal. What about after the long winter when you finally can open your windows and breathe in the fresh air. But is it fresh or is it toxic? They never touched on the omissions from the airplanes. What are we breathing in? It was like talking to the air. An empty space. And that was another thing the hypocrisy and the deception so blatantly displayed. Yet so many oblivious and accepting the elephant in the room.

Obviously, this still is a big source of contention for me. For I have written about this and now still writing about this. For I believe in transparency, taking care of and caring for others. I still care even though I have removed myself. What are we to expect from big government depends on the small governments' compliance? And vice versa. But I do worry. I want the people who bought my little cottage to have no regrets. I want my neighbors who raised their children in this neighborhood not to be victimized. It was bad enough what happened to me. Those at the top, should stop the madness. If they cannot. Then they should step down. They can start by lowering the taxes. Stop their wasteful spending and their foolishness that only wrecks and distracts causing further havoc.

When elected into a service position. You serve with the best of your ability. That is an honorable position, make it worth-while for the good of others. Wasn't that the original purpose. Not a steppingstone to further your status or glorify yourself worth. Big money is never the resolution or solution, but lack of can start a revolution. When things are done in haste, leads to government waste. There is such a thing as growing too big, too fast will create another crash. We need to stop being impressed by the wealth because the love of that—becomes stealth. When do we learn to say enough?   When we have given enough but there is always the want of more.

I've said enough. On this subject. Now I will address my stress laden life. Who would ever believe that this would be me? For I was going to be a singer, dancer, artist and missionary. Incorporating my gifts and talents that came naturally into my life. And, it did. Not in the way that I expected. But was and will always be in my life somehow, someway and in the right time. I've also always believed given enough time and through understanding the right thing would eventually be done. For problems need to be addressed, not tucked away or hidden from view or ignored as if unimportant.

At times I felt I was completely alone, stranded left to fend for myself against predators—the mercenary kind.in every form and from every direction. The love of money turns into greed. While those have lost turns to desperation of another kind. Either way there is a desperation for more. More to feed their greed. And those who need to provide in desperate times. Either will change one's character. The willingness to sacrifice without a thought to anymore. And those who have suffered losing their homes, their security their dignity too. For how much can one take before we break. We are only human. Yet, I thought we were better than this.

Just before I moved, people around me were struggling from their loses that they were never able to rise above. Or make it through those tough times. For those in control were out of touch and had their own agendas. Those who were struggling had no one to turn to for financial aid, or guidance. Without a price to pay. But they couldn't get a break. They weren't in the right place. Caught in a web, struggling for help. Trying to break free. And still, Years later, no better for those who trusted too much. Maybe held back and didn't speak out. For they still trusted in the innate goodness of man. But corruption and dysfunction crept in and stayed too long. So long. Those who profited from these times were not willing to let go, of the tight reigns of their control. Not just the money anymore, but the power bought and brought an addictive state of being. The problems that grew, the solution was always the need for more money. When money was always the root of the problem. For the wasteful spending in high places became so exaggerated and out of control creating more and bigger problems. Not knowing when to stop or how to begin to address. No one would stop this mayhem for they invested too much to turn back now. Meanwhile those struggling continue to lose more. Amidst the reckless disturbances offering no hope of reprieve.

When I learned that I would no longer have money to give relief. To help those I had grown to know. Know their history. The circumstances before and after the stumble and fall. How could that be? I paid too much for my little house. I addressed these problems immediately. But was ignored. Dismissed. That was a red flag right there. Something shady going on when impossible to reach the originator. I was determined to restore this little house back to dignity. And, I did. Inside and outside. All became a labor of love. But all those years that I fixed and repaired and restored was done amidst the brokenness. And, the ever-rising taxes even though inflation was greater than expenses and many times the income made. The government needed to be paid the greater share. Income taxes. Property taxes. Taxes on this and taxes on that. Out of the frustration, laws were made for what purpose or whose purpose? How can we feel safe when firearms are given more credence that human life? When dangerous drugs are accessible and profitable too. That doesn't make sense. But reeks of something sinister, unholy and eroding. In so many ways. I'm thinking of the people who in desperation—where who do they turn to for assistance? Before going over the bridge of troubled waters.

For years, I held on by a thread. Thanks to the slight increase in my maintenance provided every two years. I was able to make it through. I was one of the lucky ones. But, seeing the struggles around me, the ongoing worries and despair was something I could not ignore. From those whose purpose was to break and take. And find a way to profit From their mistakes. Emotionally that took its' toll. I could not understand. When I put so much in. Not to profit, but out of preservation, respect and dignity. I didn't expect to be at status quo. When those around were safe and sound in the fiduciary area of life. What was the difference? And what and who made it so? I want to know. I needed to know for months after, for those who should have been given restitution--never got a break in their circumstance of life. In the time of troubled waters and disturbing financing structure.

April 24th 2019 I do have to write about a pivotal turning point after my move on the 13th day of March. I hadn't been feeling that well for a while but contributed those feelings not necessarily unusual as I did just move. Not knowing if it was just getting through that period of adjustment, plus I still had lingering effects that I dismissed. For it was time that I should be getting stronger. Better than this. After all, I lived such a healthy life—progress was never an issue. I knew I was getting better. I slept fitfully that night. Would awake during the night questioning myself, "Was I sick. My head felt unusual but so tired I   would fall back asleep. When I awoke in the morning, I felt unusually weak. When I got out of bed, I felt unsteady. My first thought was I had vertigo. I found it difficult to walk. At least, to walk in a straight line. I felt a weakness throughout my body. I could not understand, why my body kept veering to the right. There were times, I needed to go left. So then like a circle.

What in the world is this? Am I still getting used to this condo living? For it wasn't perfectly straight. I was a little wary of eating or drinking anything. I didn't want to get sick on top of everything else. I decided it wouldn't hurt to call my doctor. After my long illness, I should have a list. But what kind of doctor that would be this knowledgeable? I remembered my last doctor that I would see before my move. I found his number and called his office.

His polite receptionist answered the call. I asked if I could talk to Dr. Merlin Brown. (like a magician) She told me he was busy at this moment. I was trying to sound nonchalant. I told her that was okay, just have him call me when he's free. Then she tells me, why don't you tell me what is going on? I told her about waking up to weakness, my strange sensation in my head and I couldn't walk in a straight line. That's all I had to say. Then she tells me not to hang up. I'm going to talk to the doctor right now. He will probably want to talk to you. I'm thinking, Oh, dear. What did I do? Was this spell something I don't want to know or even to hear?" Dr. Brown was one of the doctors that helped me when I had that strange virus, illness or malady. It was something I had never had before. The doctors I saw were stymied, sometimes giving me a medicine. That I would have to quit taking—for allergic reactions of some kind.

I learned Dr. Brown was an internist, recommended to me. I liked his easy manner. We both believed in preventative. He took all my vital signs. Had me walk. Afterwards, he told me that I should have an M.R.I. done for precautionary measures. I was surprised when he told me that he was going to schedule an appointment that morning. I had that done. I should have gone back to his office, but I was told it would take a while. So, I went home. But first I did a few errands since I was feeling pretty good. I actually drove myself to the doctors' office. I wanted to feel normal. I didn't want my body or my mind to deteriorate. I said a prayer to help me get through this. Send my guardian angels to help and protect and a prayer of thanks. For this could have been worse. When I got home, I rested a bit and waited to hear back. No news is good new I'm thinking.

152   Because, I was unusually tired, I went to bed with no problems. Kind of weak or a delicate state. I was thinking I'll call the office to find out the results of the test at 9:00 am. A little before 8:00 the phone rings and I can see it is from the lobby downstairs. "Patti this is Karen from Dr. Browns' office. We've been trying to reach you. We tried all day yesterday and tried in the evening. Do you have a new number?" I give her my new number. For when I moved to my condo Xfinity insisted on giving me a new landline number. I told them, that would complicate my life. And, it did. I told Karen I would buzz her up. But she told me that she had to get back to the office. "When we hang up be sure to call Dr. Browns' office it's important. He wants to speak to you." I tell her I will do that. Dr. Brown answered immediately. And he explained what had happened. He told me, "at first I thought you might have and inner ear problem. But from what I observed, and I didn't want to tell you at the time, "that you might have had a mild stroke." I didn't like hearing that. But he emphasized the mild, so that made me feel better. Can you come to the office this morning? Yes, I was determined to get better as soon as possible.

I would veer to the right when walking. But I noticed in the car, since I was contained, seat belt and enclosed in the car. I could drive perfectly fine. I get to the office and we went over the informational chart for any new changes. Dr. Brown explained the results of the M.R.I., there was just a small amount of bleeding on the left side of my brain. But it affected my right side. That is why I would veer to the right. I had a couple of other tests done. I was fortunate that my stroke was so mild. That I didn't need rehabilitation therapy but in less than two weeks, I will have a cognitive testing done. Which supposedly takes four hours. Recently, I asked Dr. Brown why I would get so tired. He told me even though my stroke was mild, or small I still needed more rest. I think I can do that. Maybe. I'll try.

This was a wakeup call for me. Not to push myself over the brink. We talked about stress. For my life has been stress laden. We all have a certain amount of stress in our life. In fact, the good stress is what keeps us going, alerts us when needed, and motivates us to get the job done. Adrenaline kicks in and we go beyond what we thought we could do. But there is such a thing as negative, bad stress or too much stress. So, listen all of you who are always supercharged and so proud of it. When operating on overload. Just being on the edge is a thrill you crave. To the point of being unaware of the havoc and chaos and the wreckage from the thrill of it all. Testing yourself and testing others too. Testing the limits. How much can one take, even pushing to the edge. Sometimes, they don't make it. Just because you love it. And, that has become your mode of operation brought your successes in the ruthless world of finance and other arenas as a sport. There should be boundaries set in place and accountability when misplaced. Followed up with restitution to those who suffered the consequences of such actions that spoil and plunder. Makes one wonder. What ever happened to common sense?

This could have been a horrific experience for me. When I talked to Dr. Brown, he didn't panic or scare me. He was calm and reassuring. That helped me alleviate my own fears. But he did tell me, he wanted to see me once more. When a doctor or any professional jumps to a conclusion before knowing the history or seeing the big picture, will put one in a panic state. Which doesn't help anyone. So, I believe in calm and serenity even amidst a storm. I was fortunate to have a doctor that went beyond when I was unreachable, because of my new number. So, what a good doctor I have. I am thankful. He gave me the attention needed, connect and service provided. Thank you, staff and Dr. Merlin Brown. And, thank you God for all the good people in my life for I am grateful. Now, I can continue with writing my third book. Let the journey begin. Let it be good for all.

Angel Tree

We had to prepare the area and dig the hole to fit this little angel tree, that would grow to one day be majestic, in appearance not necessarily in height. Since trees were Billy's specialty this little angel tree was in good hands. He told me to be sure that this little tree was well hydrated for the winter. Nature must have been listening, because we had tremendous snow that winter along with a very wet spring. Summer too. He's just a tree, but a symbol of abundance of nurturing and care. And always with love.

Angel Tree & Me

Several arborvitae trees had to be removed. Not just the tree but the roots also. When the row of arborvitae was removed in the front yard. It was a tremendous change. It would take a while to acclimate with the open space that really let in the sun coming up from the east. I knew I would be moving one day. I wanted to leave a special tree for the new owners. Billy and I found the perfect size angel tree at Tangle Town Nursey. We brought it back to the house and planted this tree ever so carefully. The boughs of this tree, drapes to the ground. The branches of soft pine needles can be trained to wrap around as if mediating. The top looks as if a head with long pine needles of hair. As it grows taller, this angel tree will have a majestic and reverence appearance. Right now, he's just a toddler tree or little angel tree. Me and my little angel tree. This is a present for new owners and neighborhood. Planted with love.

chapter 19
MAKE US WONDER?

Life is a journey. We plant the seed, tend to the needs to nourish and watch grow. We protect from the elements, when getting too cold we cover to protect from the chill. When getting too hot or dry we provide water and nourishment. If this was a perfect world, we all would be and do the right thing. Never a thought of harm to anyone in anyway. That is our innate consciousness, a knowingness a deeper knowledge that we all do have. At least, once upon a time. As a plant grows with the right care and conditions providing beauty, fruits to share, providing shade on a hot day and leaves that filters and cleans the air. Everything on earth is for a reason and purpose including the smallest pebbles, to the smallest ant and amoebas so tiny can't be seen with the naked eye. Everything and everyone, was made and born for a reason greater than we know or understand. For that reason alone, we must provide the best environment, nourishment and care possible. And we take loving care.

When a problem arises, address immediately. Don't let it grow to out of control. Be careful what we let in our mind our thoughts for seems to be no filters to shield and protect. We are at the mercy of who is ever in control. Not necessarily the best interest at heart. That is what happens when the consciousness becomes too cloudy, distracted and overwhelmed with excess in every form. Sensory overload from all directions. Becoming another distraction and annoyance that we just accept. For it is a right that came with a price. To lead the way or astray. What does it matter how we will be affected, headaches, earaches, stomach aches too? Excess in any form is harmful. Why can't we recognize that problem? Are we in too deep, not processing properly? On overload. Or too impressed to address. Don't be. Stop for a minute. Sometimes we need to reevaluate our priorities. How we feel at the end of the feat? That became a tour de force or is a faux pas? Try listening to our consciousness and be more aware of the senses that will help guide us. Even alert us and prepare us. Sometimes we need to change our behavior or our way of thinking. Listen a little more closely. Observe interactions and reactions. As if really learning a new way of understanding all over again. As a new language. Intelligence is just one part. Our awareness or cognizance is equally valuable. Our spirituality will guide us and bring peace to any situation. There are so many natural gifts given that enhances every ones' life. Being aware of our gifts is the key. Always.

158

March 20th a few days after my mild stroke, I must have been in a contemplative state of mind or being. For I had written. I knew my life would have been different. If my world would have offered more time, encouragement, and understanding. Knowing the importance to be heard, appreciated, and valued in the arts. To be in a creative world that inspires to bring out the best. I did want to be a singer, dancer, artist and missionary. To give back. For I knew being in that creative element was sheer happiness. Oh, to be surrounded by the love of music bringing revelry and joy, healing and escape to a wonderful place. And to dance to the rhythms. To the rhythm of life, also brings life to a party and relief from a challenging day. For the love of music / dance can transport you to another time and place. Emotions needing to be felt, sometimes as a healing or sometimes as an escape. Almost like a vacation of sheer joy and freedom to be. To be creative, is to add structure and beauty to life in your home, at work or workplace. Painting a seascape that you felt not possible. Or paint a self portrait or a portraiture. Try it. You might be amazed at what you can do. It is all in seeing the lines, the depths and subtle shadings. Smoothness and textures. How can that be achieved? Bringing it all together.

Replenishing our mind, body and soul. We all need that natural release and relief. Not from a pill. Not from a bottle. Not from a substance that was meant for profit first. See if it works. Give it a try. It might take a while. Maybe a bit unsavory. Probably not the best. First let us get by. We need to make a profit. Sorry if it's at your expense. Or your risk. That's not nice. Certainly not right. But it's the bottom line you know. That makes it so. Profitable for the revenue. The numbers you know. Can make or break. It's up to you. Allowances made can make your day. Or lead us astray. What about our quality of life we say? That's up to you too. If you obey and look the other way. Say nothing. Do nothing. And don't make waves. Maybe it's time, to address and correct. No longer impressed when looking around seeing the mess that was left unchecked. Isn't it time we change things around? Responsibility and accountability will be renown. Isn't it time we set the record straight? Instead of profiting off reckless mistakes. Let's try a more humanitarian and honorable way. Fair and square and hurts no one.

How can I incorporate these latest events into the last pages of this book? For I do care but after all these years, am I to be the keeper of those who are in need? Who comes to my door in desperation? The strange thing is these people do have family here. They've grown up here. They are hard working. I can see the intelligence behind the facade they carry with them that hides the disappointment, struggles and shame. The hardships that have beaten them down. They try and find a way out of their plight, someone they can talk to, encourage them and see the other side— that once was. When times were on their side. Those walls hide and hold back, instead of lending a helping hand. Or treated with dignity and respect when noticing a job well done. It doesn't hardly happen anymore. We live in a time of disconnect, insolated and protected from the outside world that we want to avoid. And when confronted we run and hide. Pretend we didn't see or know. How could that be? There is no reason their problems escalated instead of finding a solution years ago. These are just two predominant individuals.

Billy has done work for me at my house. He used to have his own tree service company. He had his own trucks and all the equipment necessary for his business. He also did snow removal in the winters and various other jobs throughout the season. He came to my door on a very cold late afternoon. Now, I had tons of snow on my roof. This would be the first time in my life that I would learn about snow removal on the roof. Billy came to my door saying he could remove that snow. I said okay. I thought he would come back with his crew. Instead he came back with the supplies that was needed to remove the snow. How could anyone do this solo. By the time he finished, it was dark. I paid him. And, he said, "I'm coming back tomorrow to remove the snow from the sides of your house. There was something about his manner, that I knew he kept his word. He came back the next day to remove the snow close to the house. For in the spring when snow started melting—could be a problem. It took a while to remove that snow. But he was neat about his work. The snow off the roof and mounds of snow away from the foundation of my house. Now looked secure, almost magical. I paid him his sum of money. He thanked me. As he's walking back to his truck. He turns around and says, I'll come back this spring to trim your trees.

That was my introduction to Billy, I wrote more about Billy in my second book. He did a tremendous amount of work for me. Sure enough, when spring came, and I was coming home from errands or maybe tennis. I pulled in the driveway and there was the skinniest man I have ever seen. Swinging from the branches of the river birch tree in my back yard. Well if that wasn't entertainment or I should say accomplishment this was it. I was a little apprehensive about this skinny man. Whenever he came over, he would finish a job that was needed and if he saw something needed fixing—he would just do it. Without asking or telling me. But I could see the work that was done. He did for me, because I treated him with dignity.

His fiancé had died around the time of the collapse of the economy. He went into depression. During that time, he also lost his small business. That spiraled him further down the rabbit hole. His world falling apart. Lost hope and his will. When Billy first came to my door was the beginning of a return to reason and purpose. His journey was a very winding and rocky road. His financial struggles continued. He lived up north. But most of his business was near the cities. When he needed money, I would find work for him to do. There were times, he hadn't eaten for days. I would give him food and send him home with a supply of food. I hadn't heard from Billy for a while. Thought his business must be picking up. That was not the case. He called one day, telling me he was in jail. Would I please, bail him out.

Then there was my artist friend, extremely gifted. She was a single parent with a special needs' child. She painted murals (sometimes I would paint also) at my Lake Point Condo home. Artists love their work. Painting large murals requires strength. Just setting up the structures to get to the high places would take knowledge, in itself took skill. She painted canvas also. But was known for her murals. That was also where the big money came in. I knew Susan since 2000. Since I painted and I had all this incredible wall space in my condo at Lake Point, my friend Gunnar felt I should meet Susan.

161

I remember the first time I met my artist friend. Gunnar and Susan came to my condo house. Gunnar had the most fascinating background from his childhood, to his army experiences and life itself. He was born in Sweden. His manner and speech were evident for he was smart with a sense of humor. He would bring people together and had the ability to see what was needed and what had to be done to achieve or accomplish this feat. He could be bold. He could be fearless. But he always had a big heart for others. There was also occasional doubt or insecurity would arise when unprepared from the unknown or unexpected. I believed that stemmed from his past experiences as a child and continued until adulthood. Innate, for this is not a perfect life when we are unaware. Others many times, will take advantage when knowing the amazing capabilities but also the vulnerabilities.

Upon meeting Susan, she had the presence of an artist. Even to be the subject of artists. On introduction she was warm and soft-spoken. Very alert, aware, gracious, and captivating. As an artist, she appreciated the natural lighting in my surroundings. We did have a wonderful greeting and meeting. She was working at the time on a grand mural at Lake Calhoun Beach Club, where I just moved from. It was an ongoing project for a business tycoon wanting his own place. His own space. Hide away or get away. He commissioned Susan to do murals in each room. Each room would have their own theme. All the walls, floors and ceilings. It was quite the undertaking. The thing is, the closer to finalizing this big project, the person she was working for became more demanding and obsessive. Holding back money to buy supplies needed. Now also to make the draperies for certain windows. I was concerned for her. Feeling that he wanted more from her than she was willing to give. She went beyond already with this massive project of endless murals. She didn't need or want to be part of a triangle that would only complicate her life.

During this time, there was so much going on in my own life. I had just moved, so getting settled. There were unexpected court hearings to attend from the Big D. that was ongoing, complicated my life and such a distraction. My daughter was getting married and because of my experiences I was writing my first book. I was compelled to write. Yet, torn in so many different directions. While amidst it all, I would meet Susan. Occasionally we would get together with talks of transforming certain walls throughout my condo. The more we talked, the more we would be inspired to make my condo house into a wonderland of sorts. Inviting passageways leading around the corner, in a small powder room and leading into the kitchen. We could paint a mural on that wall that leads to the eating area that overlooks Cedar Lake. A continuations of the terracotta tiled floor, incorporated into paths leading into floral gardens heading to a majestic fountain that sprayed water high above. Behind the fountain would be a plethora of colorful flowers on the hill side looking down seeing tree lines streets and tops of houses scattered about. This street represented Dean Parkway in a distant time. But to the left, we incorporated Cedar Lake. For, when standing in the kitchen, from the large corner windows in the eating area we could see Cedar Lake. We both were excited and inspired to bring the outside in. My condo house was being transformed into Old World Wonder. Looked rather European. I like that.

This was a time of accomplishments, freedom to do and be for Susan and for myself as well. In this time Susan was basically a free agent. Nothing to hold her back for she wasn't married, didn't have children. But it seemed the dynamics of the business matters, would come into play. Not always in Susan's favor. If a project grew outside the budget. Seemed Susan was the one that carried the cost at her loss. Also, seemed in the final stages the client conveniently would leave town. But looks great. We'll pay you when we get back. Meanwhile there were bills to be paid and other expense on a shoe string budget. And, of course the unexpected happens that dips into the finances. Always playing catch up. I should say paying to catch up. For there is always the interest to be paid.

Back then, it is possible to live like that. But Life changes for everyone. There comes a time when dreams of having a baby, a child. The thought grows. But the time is running out. Susan would meet a charismatic man. A man who seemed to share the same passions as she. They would have a wedding, but not really. Just a symbol. Symbolic of love, hopes and dreams a future together. But something was awry. Susan sensed it. I'm sure others felt it too. Something was amiss. It appeared to be. As a play set in motion for all to see. Or believe. It was a memory and nothing more.

163

She was with child, the early stages of her pregnancy. Therefore, with grace. Already life has become a little off track, a little more complicated. Never quite as spontaneous as before. Now a need to be responsible for her child would be born. Life was no longer about self. But giving of herself. To love and care for a baby becomes the main priority. Susan would talk of her own mother who had just returned from France. She was working for Ernst & Young overhauling the IT(information technologies) wing; capturing the eye of the French company, Cap Gemini, who then underwent full acquisition of this spectacular IT wing. And immediately hired her to perform the full installation in France. Susan was beyond proud of her mom. Who came back home to be with Susan. I was happy about that. For Susan needed her mother at this time.

I also felt a sadness and concern. For her mother would not have long to live. While in France she was diagnosed with breast cancer that had mastitis to her brain. She was not responding well to her treatment. Now was the time to be with her daughter. She would have her first grandchild. I met Susan's mom. She was living on the third floor of a historic Victorian home on Lake Harriet. I liked her. She spoke softly but distinctly. I would listen carefully to hear if she now acquired a hint of French accent in her speech. I thought she did. Just a hint and ever so softly. She was an elegant lady even in her frailty. But the wonder of it all, during this time of living with her daughter Susan—her cancer went away one hundred percent.

Susan was a loving daughter. She would take her mother for walks around Lake Harriet. Probably not all around for Susan was getting further along in her pregnancy. I know they would take architectural walks into the town of Linden Hills. Maybe stop at a local coffee shop. And if it was the right time of day or evening, there might be music at the Lake Harriet Bandshell. Of course, her mom lived so close. She would be able to hear from her own stately place. I worried at times, when Susan would tell she would have to first bring her mother's wheelchair down the three flights of stairs. Then go back to help her mother down the stairs. That made me nervous for her. And her mom. But even though getting bigger each day with her pregnancy, she felt she was strong enough. Everything was going to be fine. She was strong and healthy.

One day soon after, I received a call from Susan. She was at the hospital. She had gone into labor after taking her mom for her daily walk. For some reason, she was walking faster than usual. And, while pushing her mom up this small hill. Just a small incline. She started getting pains. She brought her mother safely home with some help from those around. She wanted to let me know her baby was born. There was some testing going on. Susan's baby was born a beautiful baby girl. Accept, her baby girl was born with down syndrome. If anyone knows about children who have this condition. They know of the problems, but they also know of the exceptional traits that many times are predominant. The early years needs are of special and attentive care. One of the main characteristics are their gentle and loving nature. So, a blessing. Susan, now a single mother with an added incentive, inspiration and determination to succeed. After all, she is a woman. She is strong and capable. But we can't do this life alone.

When I was writing this part about my artist friend Susan. I realized, I had to go into a little more depth for understanding and a clearer picture. For a better background. For we are not just the present. We are part of the events in our life that shapes us, sometimes define us. And sometimes, will change us and even redirects us. Making it even more important to always stay healthy in mind, body and spirit. And to be aware of our own self. Our own frailties. To be surrounded by people who truly care. Not because we are a steppingstone to their desires, careers or hidden agendas. We have been given these gifts and it is times like these we depend on each other to be there, to offer support when needed and know we are not alone. For there is a higher power guiding us. In those moments of need and gratitude.

Well that was the background. Hopefully for understanding. We are only human. We will make mistakes. We put our trust many times in the wrong person, for the wrong reason. Forgetting our purpose. But we do continue to live and learn. Billy and Susan were people that came into my life I know for a reason and purpose. They both have survived losses, heartaches, disappointments and struggles. that seems difficult to understand. Because, like I said or have written about— they lived here in Minnesota all their life. They have family here. Aren't we supposed to protect our own? If we are no longer capable, how can we help those in distress throughout our world? Where is the role model or mentor for others to help and guide through the rocky terrain of life, into a state or place of dignity, refinement, and inspiration. To be ready and prepared for their journey.

When I thought the worst was over, I received a distressing call from Susan. This happened over a month ago and it is now September 1rst. 2019, Labor Day. She was fighting back tears and frustrations as she is trying to tell me what happened. I'm trying to stay calm myself. What I had learned there was a court hearing concerning visitation rights of the father to her daughter that Monday.

The new judge overruled the judgement that a year and a half ago was put in place. Her eleven years old daughter was now to have equal parenting. Susan was beside herself. The original ruling resulted from the father's neglect, anger, addictions of alcohol and drugs, cocaine and whatever else. I don't know. The father worked as a bar tender in a relatively upscale bar / restaurant. From the time of Tahlia's birth, he was never consistent with his monthly payments to his child. Therefore, creating another hardship for Susan. Plus, another red flag regarding his sincerity or ability to care and parent his child. That a judge could disregard these omissions is disturbing and should be questioned. For…

"The main reason, for the first hearing was upon learning that Tahlia had suffered abuse from his girlfriend. That explained the behavior from Tahlia after each visit. It would take days for her to recover, but upon learning it was time for another visit to her father. She would protest so vehemently that Susan had to take notice. Now, this is an eleven years old child with down syndrome. Going through anything like this is unbelievable and unspeakable. Why would a judge overrule—when learning or knowing the history? The father was supposed to have drug testing done—but neglected to do so. Evidently, the court's decision didn't have much impact or influence on the father to change his ways."

Now Susan was back on the treadmill. Reliving the experiences of the past. Going nowhere. I tell Susan to go to the medias about this outrage. Write a letter to the courts explaining, the ongoing stress this has caused you and your child. Then she told me she needed money. For, she had to pay the attorney. Going to court was taking away from her work—affecting her pay. She was behind in her bills. "Susan, Tell the courts this also. They need to know." She implores, "I can't. They will think I'm an unfit mother. That I can't take care of my own child." Did Susan truly believe this? I would think that the courts would be the first one to go to for protection. Especially for matters such as this. If this is the case, that a mother who fears for her child, now to be concerned about the courts ability to take her child from her. She is the mother who loves her child. The constant force and provider, nurturer from the beginning.

I would learn this. History repeating itself, within the same time frame. Problems grew that should have been addressed years ago. Now bigger, bolder testing the limits once more. What is happening when the perpetrator has more rights and protection than the victim? We have more courts and attorneys than any other country. As if another form to profit from schemes or endeavors. To build their revenue and establish themselves in the game. Not to find a solution but to milk it for all it's worth. Find justifiable ways to indulge in the power and profit too. I can't help but question for my experiences from working in the guardian ad litem program' to the Big D. and more. And then, all the way to the present. I did have a certain knowledge and understanding. But my funds were limited. Helping others like this, offered no returns. Because, "I will, or others like me" will help those who are struggling, but it's no longer even a tax write off. Whatever we have left after the housing crash and everything else, the funds were practically broken down to smithereens. But if we bought a yacht. There would be no problem, for we would get a hefty tax break. Who continues profiting when everyone else is scrambling?

Susan would call me, needing not only my support but I was her means to help her with her expenses. Within 24 hours later, I would also hear from Billy. With only a minute to speak. Could I please, please bail him out. He begged. He pleaded. But I was overwhelmed already with Susan's troubles. Now even a bigger quandary. I could only do so much. I would help him one last time. Does it really matter anyway? When no one really listens. Do they really care? Will I ever get paid back not just from those? Those professionals who used, abused our trust, we bailed them out. It's time they looked at the books and give back what they took.

167

I wasn't expecting to end my book this way. And, I won't. For I can only do so much. Amidst all the challenging times. Fortunately, there are incredible experiences that will outweigh the worst of the times. There are choices that we make throughout our life. That is why I will always stress the importance and value of always a healthy body, mind and spirit. For once weakened we are at the mercy of others who will use and abuse. It doesn't matter the position or status. Especially in these times of such great disparity and disconnect. To combine with sensory overload and excess in every area—some more than others, can at times be too much to bear. Especially when there are better ways. Ways that unite instead of divide. When there is respect and understanding we can work together. That shouldn't be that difficult if we worked together in unity for the betterment of all. Start at the beginning value and appreciate life, our earth and the air we breathe. We all play a part in the grand scheme of things. In the choices we make in the career path we choose.

168

Is it a company that recognizes families for that is the main impetus in anything we do? We work for a company now for the benefits. Yet, the benefits which includes the necessities in life has grown out of proportion in size of the small beginning company. They can only afford so much by the time other expenses are due. It is Wall Street, big banks that lead the way and government too. To control the outcome. Even if a beginning company is to survive and thrive. But then there is another area that is the big problem that is the rising cost of insurance. From the homes everyone owns to medical care, medicines that are needed but now for the big pharma to profit. There is something wrong and sinister in this big picture. There will be those who are not impressed with big money. They will think outside the box. They know these are manmade problems meant to control the outcome. Their purpose isn't altruistic or pure. But to feed their own addiction of more. For the love of money grows but it is never enough. To feed the government waste. Making such a mess of things. They don't want to see. They will avoid and come back when it's over.

One Solitary Blue Morning Glory

 Toward the end of summer, with many gray days and lots of rain and colder than usual temperatures. I was surprised to find a solitary brilliant blue morning glory still hanging on. I had to take a picture of the wonder of it all, still surviving amidst the enduring wind, rain and cold. Giving hope.

Sleeping Cherub

Missed my house. Missed my gardens. I didn't want to part with sleeping cherub. Always so peaceful. I brought him to my condo home. Surrounded him with not only morning glories climbing up the railing, but ferns, and flowers of various colors and kind. An, experiment for me to learn and grow and see what needs to be to make a garden in the air. I also bought air plants that is misted occasionally. I can do that. We live and learn.

chapter 20

NOT ORDINARY MOSTLY EXTRAORDINARY

From the time I knew I was going to write another book. (of this nature) The thought of delving into the past into the present was almost agonizing for me. For I really thought, my first book said it all. But, something happened, somewhere at some time in the process of getting my book out there for the world to see for themselves. And be the judge of such an endeavor as exposing the side of life, that many don't want known. But that has never been my philosophy in life. I think we all should know, especially at the right time. When we're ready to face the music or know the facts. What we are getting into? Needing to know the dynamics and repercussion that follows. I don't ever want to be clueless or put inf the dark. I don't want to be stifled not in my knowledge, my creativity or my ability.

We all should be encouraged to expand and broaden our knowledge and our interest. Not be one dimensional. Give back what we borrow in better condition than before. Whatever I did, I did the best of my ability. I think we all should do that, instead of halfheartedly. I believe in taking care of, our children our family, our community and society. The importance of giving back what we borrowed and helping others when in need. Give guidance when lost or uncertain. Be helpful in any way possible. Be aware for that to me is preventative. Provide nourishment to stay healthy with a vibrant life for yourself, your family and community. Teach whatever you know to be right, for that always served me well. I did make mistakes and still do, but it's always a learning and teaching experience for everyone. If someone said I couldn't do something—I would prove to them that I could do it. No matter how tall or small but mighty, fast and curious. Sometimes furious too. It's okay to be angry at your circumstance in life. But, always try and understand the dynamics of that experience that unglued you. That must have been more important than you realized. And, if not. Let it go. But if you can't let go for it affects you so. Address and correct. Speak up. Speak out. Sometimes we need to shout. To be heard. To be understood of what and who hurt us so. So deeply we still feel the pain.

At least we can feel. That's what it's all about. Our senses, that will bring out our common sense. What we feel. What we say and how we say it every day in every way. Practice makes perfect. Don't be shy. Don't be afraid to cry. The tone of voice will give us away do we waver and stammer or are we speechless with fear. Do we boast out loud whatever we do for we like recognition and admiration too? A little pride goes a long way. Or can sink us to the deep. Surround yourself with good people, good things, good thoughts. Bring out the good in yourself and recognize the good in others. What they do. And how they do. They are lovely but are they loving too. Do they wear a mask that hides and conceals for afraid to reveal the dark side of self when wanting to show the light to make it all right?

172

Breathe a little deeper, Step back, see what is needed observe. Look around see and hear what is needed. Start fresh compliment the day instead of adding more demands. Take time appreciate the moment for yourself and others. Job well down now, relax your mind and your body. Take time to enjoy the moment, the day. Take time to play a little, laugh a little, do a little dance graceful and smooth to the beat of the drums, or simply the rhythm of life. The ticking of a clock to a tapping of a pencil to the rhythm of a washing machine as it does it cycle. Be spontaneous for a change. Don't be so connected that you lose real contact with real people. Not an allusion. Unless it offers substance and fresh ideas and inspiration. Whatever you do, make it beautiful. Make it useful and lasting. Not just for a day, but forever and a day. Maybe always. If meant to be. Bring out the best in you and me and others will follow. That is the key.

This obviously is not a typical book. But, for so long life has been such a challenge that I had enough of my serious life. I can see what needs to be done. I can see who needs a helping hand. And it is just a simple matter of getting down to basic. What is necessary in life. And, it really does start with a strong foundation. I'm in my condo now. Starting to feel somewhat adjusted. We will see. One thing for sure, all the responsibilities from my little cottage house are no longer mine to bare. Leaving me more time to write and do more for myself. I think. I'm not quite sure yet. For I wanted to finish this book. And this space has allowed me to do with certain limitations distractions of other kinds. But that is life. I still miss my little cottage house. Even though I'm not that far. But it saddens me when I see what happens when houses are torn down replaced with big boxes, set up quickly. And very expensive too. Now no longer affordable. Caught in between. The haves and the have nots. What happens to those who need to replace what they sold to highest bidder. Inflation doesn't stop in the house market. We are the solutions now for those who want to acquire more.

173

I am going to close for now. I need to close. But I will tell you. I planted morning glories on my balcony and impatience and various other flowers. And discovered air plants. Summer is waning and is showing the effects on my flowers. I have an interesting view from my balcony. I always pretty much know what is going on to maintain the grounds to keep things in working order from sunup to sundown. The big new complex across the street from me, is now complete. A very inviting place. I love that I live so close to the church where I taught my little class for nine years. Hearing the bells from the church on Sundays, calling as a reminder of what we all hold dear to our hearts. There is a train track somewhat near, not very far at all, as I look down my balcony to see the train passing. There is an office building to the left of me. That offers another side of life. Interesting to see. Sometimes a little irritating too. My friend tells' me this morning. "There's the smoking ladies taking their smoke." Must be a necessity before they start their day. Have their break. Their afternoon lunch and their midday slump.

And of course, the end of the day—drag. Before heading for home or their workout classes. Or maybe a sprint around the lake.

I need to close. But enjoy your day. Take precious care of you and yours. Do something good for yourself and an act of kindness to someone in need. Needing a hug, friendship or a helping hand. Let's go beyond our self. Pleasantly surprise our self and others too. Take precious care. And enjoy. Don't let the stresses of life take over. There is a higher power to help us through each day. All we need to do is ask for guidance and blessings with gratitude.

Patti Zona

174   January 14th of 2019 I had written a letter to the state of Minnesota. What I had written speaks for itself. Still processing from the move of my little cottage house. I bought my house for too much money not knowing of the non-disclosed problems that became mine to bare. I restored and repaired with my dwindling funds. But, I did it. I even paid extra on the principle for all those years. I did what I was told to do to restore and try and regain the imposing losses. It did not matter to the state or those who would benefit. For I was in a vulnerable state when I sold my house that I had restored for more than I should. Not really, for if there is a problem, I will fix it, or have it repaired. Address and correct in every area of life our home, workplace or office, to corporations and wall street, clerical to clergy, and that goes for big government and applies to the small government too. Simplify and dignify not complicate into oblivion. This is what I had handwritten to the state of Minnesota…

I now had no money to put down on a house. All because of Merrill Lynch used my funds to replenish their own pockets. Well, that affected me for years. And, still does. I've written about this, "too many times." But Minnesota State doesn't care. They just want to take everything I have, without a thought or care. How could you keep doing this to me? You have become mercenaries. You don't find solutions. You create business to profit instead from these problems. You have opportunities, but you ignore again and Again. Because, you have established your teams to help conceal and steal from your forum of designer laws and rules—for yourself.

I bought a little cottage house. That was supposed to help me regain my finances. That was a cruel joke played on me. I paid too much money, but Edina Realty and Jane Paulus never disclosed the huge and expensive problems. Once again, I was ignored, becoming mine to bare. You profited many times over. But your waste and disregard were your impetus for more. I sold my house would you believe-- for the same price that I had paid for, 12 years before. And, you want even more money. Minnesota Nice. Leave me alone!

Why am I paying such high taxes? When your state of Minnesota has allowed predators and it is the white-collar criminals—the most culpable. "And there are so many—here" Who are continually rewarded, blinded by their greed or ambition and encouraged by their peers. They no longer know right from wrong. How could they? When the predators do not have to be held accountable. As long, as the money is great enough.

I've always tried to do the right thing. I care, probably too much. That is why, I am stymied when my life is filled to the brim with these ongoing "manmade" problems that have never been addressed. Do you know who my ex-husband is? And you don't question the disparity? Life continues and he does have regrets now. He's only human. So much so, that he has removed himself from the problems that were allowed to grow. My divorce wasn't fair affecting my life, my children's life also. I could continue, I have written the state several times already. I've also given this state two of my books. So, this is on the record. The history and challenges when facing financial adversity here in this state. I've been misplaced and replaced too. I wasn't born here. Obviously, that was my problem. But I have lived here long enough and endured enough and helped your state, pro bono, volunteering too many times. You should be thankful or grateful to me instead of draining and disappointing me.

I can't believe what you ask of me. If you want or expect me to pay such exorbitantly high taxes. Then go after all those predators—Merrill Lynch, Edina Realty. I won't name them all—now. But don't you know, realize or understand I could pay those high taxes and gladly. But I can no longer afford to do so. My family has grown. I now have eight grandchildren. I have friends who were drastically affected by the fallen and failing economy. How can I help them? How could they have lost so much and not be able to rebound from their losses. But the banks greedily stepped in. This was their time to profit once again. As well as others. Like many others they were told to go bankrupt or sell their house to the bank. Always in the banks favor.

There were times I tried to help my friends and those who were struggling. But made impossible to even do this. It wasn't my position to help financially, but in their times of desperation. I did try and provide some financial help. Until, the sale of my little cottage house took me to no return. Minnesota you ask the impossible from me and others. When you expect me to pay or subsidize your wishes, pay for facilities in the time of despair and blatant disparity. You profit off of addictions of all kinds, instead of teaching and practicing preventative and promoting healthy standards. You encourage bad behavior or unhealthy behavior—profit from them too. Legalizing gambling, opioid addictions and other dangerous drugs in abundance. And don't get me started on profiting from the NRA. The big YUK.

Enough and I've said enough, and you've taken enough. Wednesday I am seeing my tax man. But I cannot comfortably fill out all my personal financial information. First, it really isn't that great. But I'm sure you already have my records. Just know. You will get your money that you feel you are owed. I am the one who has lost more so much, without any thought or care from your state. While others have profited splendidly. Don't you ever question your role in the disparity? Then how and why.

Aren't you even curious about the cause or effect? Have you ever thought about investigating and discovering and getting to the root of these problems? Instead of accepting acts of injustice. Try preventing, stepping in or stopping the aberrant behavior. Try encouraging and having higher standards instead of being swayed by big money. Promote healthy and clean living instead of coddling and rewarding bad behavior. Teach right from wrong. Encourage and inspire for greatness instead of promoting stealth and mediocrity. I never expected to pay such high taxes for all these years. I thought you would wake up and question. That never happened. I no longer can trust you or the governing of this state. For you don't care about the reason or purpose. It's the revenue and power gained for you. I live off of my alimony or maintenance what ever you call it. Because of Merrill Lynch I no longer have that cushion for the unforeseen expenses. Every two years, I do receive a small 1% to a 2% cost of living increase. But inflation grows higher and high taxes takes most of it. I do not own two homes or more. I have my condo where I moved in last August of last year. I try and cut back and well as many others. But you always keep wanting more. Enough for now.

177

I bought this wonderful note paper, that had different quotes on each page. This was apropos "What do we live for if not to make life less difficult for each other?" by George Eliot and "One life on this earth is all that we get, whether it is enough or not enough and the obvious conclusion would seem to be that at the very least, we are fools If we do not live in as fully and bravely and beautifully as we can." by Frederick Buechner

That quote was on the paper when I had written this letter to the state. I will add "May we all continue to live and forgive, learn our lessons well that we not repeat histories mistakes. It's time we work together united in purpose. Not divided once more."

Many occurrences today should not even be an issue. But has been man made-- out of greed. Dysfunction and corruption for so long has become accepted, another obstacle, another barrier and means to feed the greed.

Everybody needs a home. That has always been the American dream.

Patti Zona

Miniature Red Rose Still Standing Tall

I had written before, in another place, space and time, upon seeing the last blooms of summer. All the awakening of feelings, almost nostalgic. Wanting to preserve this space in time. But we all know, time waits for nobody. But we can sill preserve what is lasting and good. Plant the seed.

March 10, 2018
ABOUT LIFE AND TAXES

I found a small journal with a typewriter on the cover. I opened it and read, "It's December of 2016. I have been sick for over 3 months". It was interesting, because over the course of those months I wrote—describing the symptoms that would change from day to day, week to week. Some were vague, but a nuisance for I knew something was not going well, not right. For, I have always lived a healthy life. To be feeling this way for so long was telling me something was going wrong. I could eat the right foods. I have always been active having healthy interests. I did a painting during this time—thinking it would create a new mindset focusing on my gift of creating once more. My life has been filled with stress for so long, I felt the weight of all those problems beginning to take its' tole. I finished that painting—a beautiful lion with an amazing mane and gentle features not fierce at all. But, rather symbolic—to stay strong in my convictions to overcome obstacles to learn and grow through my experiences. If it be for the good—of all.

There were only three pages on the journal that I had written. I had stopped in January of 2017. I was still sick—my symptoms with relentless pain making it impossible to sleep or exist though the day. This went on for months. The doctors were puzzled—going from one doctor to the other. For, doctors are specialized now. Needless to say, taxes prevailed. I did not have the thought or cognizance of time or numbers. I paid what I could but was limited with my funds. Meanwhile, my books were beginning to get serious attention from publishers—all over, every where and anywhere. I had pretty much given up. I wrote to make a difference and to awaken the conscience. The new interest, once again gave me   reason, purpose and hope. Maybe, whatever time I have left—will make that difference.

During this time and for so many years, my life was stress ridden. I knew that too much stress eventually does take a toll on mind, body and the soul too. I would have to extricate myself from the problematic areas. That is hard to do—when opportunists from all shapes and sizes, stature and positions are waiting in the wings for their time to test their limits and gain their opportunity. For they knew that the moral compass was becoming non-existent. They could and would wait patiently for they had their team, their crew and the means to develop or execute their plan. The laws were in their favor—with new designer laws to help pave the way to guarantee their successes. The bottom line, their quota or numbers are their incentive without a thought or care to those who have already lost too much. When is enough—enough? We can't ask that question enough times when the problems keep growing bigger, wider and wilder too. Now we ask the question, "How and when did all these problems grow to this magnitude? Now becoming incomprehensible—unimaginable, complicated and convoluted.

As I was looking for the numbers plus time line for my taxes. There were other factors besides my deteriorating health. During that time, I changed my banking from US Bank to BMO Harris bank. US Bank was the only bank I had ever worked with in my life. I believe was the right decision to change my banking for obvious reasons. But, it took a while to have my proper checks made. Therefore, I didn't have my transactions recorded in sequence for a short while, but just enough to disrupt my routine. I changed my accountant or my tax man, my bank and I was set to sell my house. All about the same time. Alone making these decisions, thinking that I had to start fresh would be enough to heal me. Not rational. for, I still was not well enough to really process the significance in these decisions in desperate times. Oh, yes. My book too was finally taking an interest—meaning I was one of their main targets or possibility. The demands—time and expenses kept growing. Meanwhile, my life continues in a haze of uncertainty.

Jim, I am going to stop here. But, I will continue with addressing, "why I couldn't find all the numbers." Knowing the history is the key to understanding. My life has become a commodity for others profit. That doesn't reassure me in this state of Minnesota—where it all began...I'll write further for understanding. It's not always black or white. It's not always about the numbers. But the cause and effect or getting to the root of the problem. The discovery and then doing what is right. Having solutions instead of creating or making another business off of the problem or broken-ness. I will try and stay on track with my search.

Patti Zona   612 926 82191

Continuation...

It is now March 19, 2018. I'm trying to understand my life—to make sense of it all. Because, from the time I was very young, the dynamics of money was always in some way in play—allowing a purpose, cause and the affect of events around me—influencing judgment, personality, causing conflicts through control in the home, workplace, government etc. and of course Wall Street. The revenue just keeps growing in numbers, acquiring more but never enough for those empowered through their acquiring of money and financial judgements—always secured and never having to be held accountable or responsible. Creating an even larger divide beyond sensibility. In the process, insidiously losing their moral code of honor and decency. Forgotten, buried beneath the debris of broken promises, unspoken or regrets never acknowledged—not wanting to go there for ego, but in reality, not to expose their shame. We all make mistakes. It's only when we admit, address and not repeat the same mistakes that we can turn that new leaf to discovery of the importance of truths to be known, heard and understood. We can do and be better. For we all play a role from our own experiences. Are we for profit only? Are the necessities of this life about the quantity or willingness to sacrifice quality of life? I hope not. I do know this...

It is important to pay our taxes. But, when the taxes "some of us pay" are not only unfair but way excessive—eroding our quality of life. Taxes so high that it is impossible to recover from our losses—even to this day. It's been too long without a break, a thought or any relief. We all want progress that is healthy, worthwhile that inspires ourselves and others. We want to be part of the decisions that will affect and impact our quality of life and our children's future. To be part of—united in our thoughts, ideas and our actions. Are they sincere? Or, are there hidden agendas that are privy to only a select few. Relying on the expertise of those who knew enough, hopefully cared enough and hopefully capable. But, the outcome is always dubious.

Who do we trust? When the decisions made are only "Band Aids" a fix for a limited time. A screen to distract, but nothing of substance only a repeat of past rhetoric, distractions and busyness—resulting in empty promises, broken dreams and always—higher taxes. When already still financially burdened from the dysfunction and corruptive practices never addressed. Designer laws were created to protect the wealthiest and largest companies. They learned nothing, certainly not remorse. Living in a world of entitlements generates a false sense of being—always right never wrong. Regardless, if the world around them is crumbling in despair—the entitled are untouched. Too removed to understand their part in the brokenness.

184

Ever since my divorce, I have paid quarterly taxes. Why is that? Four times a year the stresses mount. Always on the mind. When I was married, we never paid quarterly taxes. My divorce was never fair in the first place. But, what would I expect when my husband loved power and money—goes hand in hand. Our divorce played out for years. The world of mergers and acquisitions / hostiles takeovers was his domain. Banking was his area of expertise. My experience was so unbelievable, I wrote a book about that experience and the aftermath…The thing is, no one in position ever questioned the blatant disregard or disparity. Strange. For all the successes were built in our marriage. Our last child would be going off to college. Seemed, the courts only looked at the millions plus that he brought in and his daring transactions that so impressed. I was a homemaker with many talents and capabilities that I brought to our home. I could do many things. Did whatever needed to be done. And, did it well.

Even after our divorce, my ex-husband would take me to court for whatever mundane reason that grew in his mind, for over ten years. During that time, there were financial predators hanging in the wings, biding their time. Waiting for their opportunity to make their mark. I know, going to court all those years had a negative affect on my life. Plus, every quarter, I would have to stop and pay my taxes. It didn't matter that these professionals in every shape and size had now become the problem, my biggest threat and adversary. They had all the advantages in the world and they knew it. When the supreme courts ruled these companies were exempt from problems the government would assist them, guide them—bail them out. Our government, our country that we were to trust and to protect us was no longer capable. For they became invincible with the new rulings protect them. Unfortunately, they grew to have no boundaries either. They no longer knew right from wrong.

I got the house. My husband never ever paid on the principle. Since, my divorce I have always had a mortgage. But, I do pay on the principle. Still, the predators kept coming. Merrill Lynch (Tom Drees) in December of 2004—I learned never put my down payment on my condo that I bought. Instead, invested the money-separately. He lost it all. And most of my money for my financial future—over $800,000.00. By the time I left Merrill Lynch, my money had dwindled to barely $200,000.00. I contacted the SEC in New York, talked to various people at Merrill Lynch, plus the Attorney General in Minnesota, probably Washington D.C. also. All to know avail. For, I was an individual not a corporation. No one to turn to for help of any kind. I wrote about that experience. To inform, empower through knowledge and understanding and try to awaken the dormant conscience.

I bought a little cottage house in October of 2006. I only had a month to move. My daughter was having her second baby. I wanted to be moved and settled at this time. But, that was not to be. I did move. But, the problems with the house were never disclosed. It was like jumping from the pot to the fire. Again, my calls to Edina Realty were dismissed numerous times. I was even threatened. I paid more for my little cottage house than my condo. Now, I had even less money. I was told I would be getting money back from the government. But, instead my taxes just kept getting larger! Every quarter! Why was this happening to me? I wrote another book about the experiences of buying this little cottage house in a time of rampant deceptive practices. The corporate mercenaries thrived amidst the financial fallouts and also all the bailouts. Testing and checking the waters to see how much they could get away with as the corporate elite before them. Dysfunction and corruption in its highest form. The busyness doesn't end and neither does the corruptive practices stop. Now, the housing market became the target as a means for profit. For everyone needs a home. Another form of business built from shaky practices becoming shaky grounds.

During this time, I finished my first book and wrote a second. I was an unknown author with two important books to be read. For important information is not always available or mentioned. Busy times. I would learn that my book / books publishing or marketing would be tested, blocked becoming an exhausting endeavor, expensive too. But, taxes do not see or understand beyond their demands of more—even when the well is almost empty. Never given the opportunity to replenish. Quarterly taxes. I don't know why I have to pay quarterly taxes—when people that have more money, means and time than I have. Just give me one good solid reason. And, do I have to do this for life? Which brings me to all my stresses between all the professional opportunist, and the wannabes surrounding me—making their presence known creates another form of stress. In the later part of 2016, I got sick. I'm basically healthy for I've always lived a healthy life style. I've written about this. Well, I ended up being sick for over a year. In fact, I was at my doctors yesterday. I told him, I was feeling stronger. He believes so too. I have to have my bloodwork drawn every month for six months. I don't like needles, but I can get over that. He did tell me, that stress is a killer. Too much over times your body becomes toxic or broken down. And one point, I was so exhausted and weak I thought I would just pass away in my sleep. I was okay with that for my life was relatively good. After all, I have 8 grandchildren. Amazing, beautiful and wonderful new lives. Smart and gifted. So, I am fortunate. But, I want to be able to enjoy these times, instead of waiting for my quarterly taxes to rear its ugly head. Sorry, but they are despicable when I no longer have the capability or the funds to pay every quarter. Thick or thin. Well or not.

I will close soon, but will add, "the only reason I could afford to pay some of my taxes was every two years, I do get a small cost of living increase. My last was a little over 1%. Nothing to brag about, but just enough to cover certain items. I haven't had a vacation in years. I help my family and friends when they are in need. That is important to me. When the economy collapsed in 2008, it actually started long before that time there was a insidious rippling affect. Not understood. The busyness of peoples lives took over, with little thought or time to consider a plan that would keep their lives solvent, another job, renting part of their house or grown children moving back home. But, also always scrimping. Very little saving if any. So tired, they accept their plight in this life here in the land of the brave and the home of the free. Why don't we say land of unity, progressive for all, wishing peace and wellbeing, Accomplishments recognized in honesty and integrity that inspires true greatness. I can only pay what I can afford in these taxes. Just make sure, my money goes for the good.

I hope this letter isn't too harsh. It's been very trying. But, that is my life at this time. I'm sure I have forgotten something. If so, let me know. We can talk or I can write a better explanation. Let's work on a better tax method. Flat tax is good. We don't need complicated and convoluted. We can expend our energy on healthier and more meaningful ways. I'm tired for now…

I do want to add, in fact I must add, there must be responsibility and accountability held to higher standards. When mistakes are made repeatedly or they use their skill, competence for their own agendas to control their own wealth or their companies wealth or go to the length to preserve their wealth along with their peers (building their teams) to prevent, block or screen to their own advantage of those less informed or privileged or less fortunate they need to be held accountable and responsible for their repeated action that caused the economic collapse in 2008. This mentality was building in the 1980's. The excitement of new growth and being part of became the impetus in corporations, banking, wall street, big government, attorneys, judges too kept their purpose tight within their circles. The economy grew along with the greed. The cost of property and housing grew to ridiculous prices. Yet, those who had it all could and would take over, their share and more, build their stash and their cash. The greed grew- taking over their thoughts and actions. The moral code of decency, ethics, common sense became buried in their sub-conscience. Those who were to be held to higher standards became the biggest problem. But they always had their team, their cohorts, for encouragement, support, to screen and appease. And, years later when all came tumbling down, starting in 2000, brewing, bubbling until no longer be contained—it was a sad and desperate time but in 2008 the bubble burst, the collapse of the economy caused a crash. The majority of people were affected the most—lost their money, their homes, left shocked and despaired.

But, those in big government made the decision to bail out those who caused the fiasco. Not with their money. But using the tax money from the people, they would shoulder the burden for years. The corporate leaders were so elated, jumping for joy. Their plan had worked. They didn't have to pay—or give back. They could continue to play—by their designer rules set for the few. To guarantee their financial wealth. Meanwhile, the majority who trusted were left to struggle, sometimes even to defend their worth, their value their virtue as they hold on to their principles, integrity and honor. Don't you know? Those are just some of the qualities in life most prized. Not abundance of this and that, the biggest and the best, the most money ever—everything a contest. Forgetting, that the growing process is the best when shared, appreciated, nurtured and cared for.

For too long, we have built this country, businesses, churches, media and etcetera on the dysfunction and corruption that became acceptable. As a role model that impresses, a flash of dash, but leaves a hole filled with debris scattered about. People are resilient. They pick up the pieces left behind. They try to rebuild, reconstruct their lives, their homes. It's not the same. It's a long process. The hurts, the recovery is a long process in itself. People moving in. People moving out. People moving away. Away from the struggles to find new hope. Try searching or reaching for the stars, the moon—to Mars or Neptune. That would bring new ideas, to relocate. Maybe this earth is a lost cause—because those in position of power and money have it all anyway. Now restless and bored. They have the means and their teams to plan their escape and erase their part, their past. They don't want to be reminded of their part in the chaos created by ignorance and unaccountability that was allowed because of rampant greed—impresses. Look around. We all play a part in what we choose to accept or ignore. Simple—if there is a problem—address it. Fix it. Repair. Restore but don't ignore. That simple philosophy applies to businesses, government, schools, churches etcetera. No one is exempt from the responsibilities in this life. We need to take care. Take care of. Take care of our children. Take care of those who no longer are capable. We need to have our dignity back and well as the money that was lost from those we trusted. They don't need it. They never deserved it. And, it set a terrible example to all—to use, to learn or not repeat the same mistakes. If you look at history, if you find the root of the problem, if you ask questions, start with the easy ones and go to where know one dares to answer. Maybe then we can do and be better for all. For we are in this world together. Not to rape and plunder, but to restore to brilliance that inspires us all to go beyond what we know. We can grow. We can allow others to grow, accomplish and achieve.

That is what we all deserve and should strive for ourselves and for others.

I think, I've said enough for now. I could touch on education, meditation versus medication, health care and welfare, sociology, psychology as well as philosophy. So many interests, directions and all needed and necessary. I could go in the sports arena, the demands and toll on the body. I could touch on hard labor, the wear and tear, repetition eventually breaks down—on anything or anyone. Regardless, we need to be aware and respectful of our limitation for ourselves and others. How much can we take before we break, physically, mentally, morally etc. That is a big problem in this land of excess and expectations sometimes too great. Awareness and preventative and mindfulness too and a certain amount of common sense does wonders. I will close for now. Any questions call me. Also, do think about those quarterly taxes. I realize there are people that love accounting, numbers, data and data entry. But, if they want quarterly taxes that can be their choice. But don't force quarterly taxes on me or others like me. You will get your tax money. But, taxes have to be fair, equitable not another added stress. That also stress their bank. I'm done for now…

Patti Zona
612 926 8219
March 21, 2018

Spring is here. Still, snow on the ground. Easter is around the corner. Hopefully the snow will melt before Easter. Would you believe Easter this year falls the same day as April Fools? Only in America…

To the Attention of Ed Kaiser,

I want to thank you for the call back. I know it wasn't easy, maybe just curious but that's okay too. At any rate, I know it wasn't easy for you--when not knowing the depth of the problem. You did call me back. That was admirable even though your knowledge was limited to one side. You at least had an interest in understanding. I realize or know, "your job is to shield and protect Edina Realty. But, that also means to keep those in your circle honest, forthright, trustworthy and aboveboard, lawful, legal and also street legal, unequivocal, fair and square, on the up and upfront." The economy was on the verge of collapse when I bought this little college house. It was in a time of the rise and the fall, on Wall Street and the housing market was hit hard and used as a means to capitalize on the information known to a select few. But, in the process would also sink to a new low. For desperation seeped in high places and every means to maintain and insure their status financially and otherwise--not to crash or succumb and crumble in the fall. To stay at the top of their game even if it now meant sacrificing long held values and principles while using the unsuspecting buyer who would cross their path in that inopportune time. What was suppose to be my solution turned out to be a financial trap where transactions made in those desperate times broke the rules and code of ethics and behavior no longer applied. I Okay, I'm going to try and keep this simple. I'm not a technical writer, so you will have to bare with me as I explain to you my experience of nondisclosure and unsurmountable and expensive problems. I addressed immediately "in every way possible" but was ignored, dismissed and treated badly. I will try and send the letters or emails that I wrote recently to Attorney General Lori Swanson etc.

Because in this past week or so, I have written so much about this little house--makes me weary. And, if it is one thing I dislike--it is repetition, right after "blatantly dishonest actions and injustices." This is unbelievable that this problem for some strange reason is ignored. Why wasn't it address? It would have saved so much grief, hardship and not to mention the stress of it all--emotionally, financially and in so many other ways for life goes on. We have no control over natural occurrences that can have devastating impact in our lives. But, when there is a lack of ethics, transparency in transactions, and the revenue becoming the main objective--then there is an eruption and erosion of ethics and standards. People who have caused "become conflicted, shady and confused not knowing right from wrong" and those who are adversely affected "no longer know who to trust." Problems need to be addressed immediately and if not there should be accountability and restitution. If people are not capable, incompetent, or have their own agenda of conflict of interest--it doesn't matter that they are a relative, naturally devious, driven by greed or filling their quotas--their destructive actions need to be addressed--clean up their act! I had written in my previous letter to Lori Swanson and Laura Flanders, about problems that are not addressed, but grow out of control, made complicated and convoluted by time and paper world. NOW, THE PROBLEM IS NO LONGER RECOGNIZABLE. That is what has happened in this case. I bought a house "for way to much money' and the problems were hidden, concealed never addressed! That is called NON-DISCLOSURE These problems should have been addressed, disclosed in order for me to make a wise decision. All of this is in the papers that I sent to the attorney general... Who has the time anyway?

192

The only thing that keeps me going with this--is the audacity of these problems being ignored for so long, keeps growing to ridiculous proportions as if some perverse joke. It's not funny. It's disgraceful and maddening. And, don't tell me, this is my problem--now. I was finishing up my first book when I moved into this little cottage house. The bed rooms upstairs were very small. Hmmm, but fortunately cute and rather inviting. The upstairs could be expanded--for a prices. But, immediately on discovery of the problems throughout this house, by the time I fixed, repaired and restored to make this house habitable I could no longer afford to expand the upstair bedrooms. Because, Jane Paulus of Edina Realty avoided me, I ended up writing my second book--a continuation of my first book. The Value of a Homemaker and Little Cottage

House--revolution and revelations. Meaning, when problems are not addressed, they don't go away. They just get bigger and those problems manifest, entangles and permeates in all parts of your life. Especially, when not addressed, ignored, becoming the untouchable or unreachable. I write to enlighten and inspire "all" people. To rise above situations that catch us off guard, astounds us, confuse and disappoint us. We learn from our mistakes not to repeat. But, what happens when those mistakes are never acknowledged and many times covered up, ignored and pushed aside until forgotten by many. Unfortunately for me or I guess fortunate. I have a very good memory. I can forgive. But, when problems grow, haunt and taunts you while eroding your finances and quality of life, I won't forget. And, until there is restitution that is acceptable, I won't let this matter drop. Oh, yes. I also write to awaken the consciousness of those who have forgotten their real reason and purpose.

Several years ago, while I was talking to an attorney from Edina Realty about this problem. Out of the blue, when I told this attorney I had spent over 200,000 dollars to fix the problems. He said, "Well, if we wrote you a check for 200,000 would that help you feel better about this situation?" I was shocked. I didn't know what to say. Of corse, it would have helped, but was this for real or was it a sick ploy or test? I never heard back from him. Life gets busy and busier. What once was catastrophic is now a jarring memory. I told you about this agent last week that was excited about selling this unique house. I never intended on staying here this long. I've put so much money in that I will never get this money back. Going upstairs--there is a nautical feel to it. The bedrooms are small, but lots of character, built-ins. Cozy in the winters. The entry or foyer is spacious especially for this era--built in 1915. Looking from the foyer--the great room with beamed ceiling is inviting, captivating with large windows looking out into beautiful gardens and pathways. I have made this little cottage house into something special, almost magical. It draws me in. Keeps me here-- even when it continues to take so much from me.

I just received a wonderful note, from a dear friend visiting. When she saw my books, she said, "Patti, where can I get your books?" I gave her both my books. In her note, she wrote that she finished both books and stated, "I was one of the bravest persons she's ever known." And, she complimented me on my books. Once she started reading--"captured her attention, like so many great books she's read." And, yes she loved the cottage house book also. That wonder note, inspired me. Empowered me also. Imagine what could or would have transpired if I had bought this house with dignity instead of betrayal. I'm exhausted but what more can I say, except we all deserve better than this.